William Humphrey

The Divine Teacher

A Letter to a Friend

William Humphrey

The Divine Teacher
A Letter to a Friend

ISBN/EAN: 9783744700511

Printed in Europe, USA, Canada, Australia, Japan

Cover: Foto ©Lupo / pixelio.de

More available books at **www.hansebooks.com**

THE DIVINE TEACHER.

A LETTER TO A FRIEND.

With a Preface

IN REPLY TO NO. III. OF THE "ENGLISH CHURCH DEFENCE TRACTS," ENTITLED "PAPAL INFALLIBILITY."

BY

WILLIAM HUMPHREY,

PRIEST OF THE SOCIETY OF JESUS.

LONDON: BURNS & OATES, LIMITED.
NEW YORK, CINCINNATI, CHICAGO: BENZIGER BROTHERS.
—
1895.

Nihil obstat.

FRANCISCUS WYNDHAM,
ex Cong. Oblat. S. Caroli, Censor Deputatus.

Imprimatur.

✠ HENRICUS EDUARDUS.
Archiep. Westmon.

PREFACE.

THE immediate cause of the publication of the following Letter is to furnish an answer to No. 3 of the English Church Defence Tracts, entitled *Papal Infallibility*.

The object of those Tracts is stated by their authors,[*] who sign themselves 'H. P. L.' and 'W. B.,' to be 'to place within the reach of readers who may not have time for deeper investigation some answers to current Roman Catholic arguments against the position and teaching of the English Church.'

To answer and explode the objections of the tract-writers is easy; but my desire is to build up as well as to destroy, and therefore I enter, not upon a polemical discussion, but upon a thetical exposition of the Catholic doctrine. This is the real and, of itself, a sufficient answer to the Tract; but it may be well that I also briefly notice its statements in detail.

It contains, among others, the following propositions:

I. That the dogma that the 'Roman Pontiff has

---

[*] It is now at any rate no secret, for it has since been elsewhere publicly stated, that the initials are those of Canons Liddon and Bright, of the University of Oxford.

full and supreme power of jurisdiction over the universal Church, not only in matters of faith and morals, but in matters of discipline and Church government, this power being plenary, and also ordinary and immediate over all and every one of the Churches, and over all and every one of the pastors and the faithful;' that 'this dogma virtually reduces the Bishops to the condition of the Pope's commissioned agents;' that 'the whole Roman Catholic world becomes his diocese, and every single Bishop in his communion is really his deputy and vicar;' that 'he is spiritually and ecclesiastically to be sole and absolute monarch;' and that 'the government of the Church becomes in his hands an autocracy.'

The tract-writers qualify this statement by a note, wherein they say, as to the dogma virtually reducing the Bishops to the condition of the Pope's commissioned agents, 'Not indeed professedly; a preceding paragraph *verbally* saves the ordinary jurisdiction of Bishops as successors of the Apostles.'

They go on to say that it 'cites a passage from St. Gregory the Great with a curious perversion of its scope.'

As to this I observe, 1. That the Catholic faith teaches that, in virtue of the primacy which our Divine Lord conferred on Peter and his successors the Roman Pontiffs, they, the Roman Pontiffs, have episcopal authority over the whole flock of God, including the Bishops as well as their subjects, the inferior clergy and the faithful—episcopal authority consisting in an immediate and ordinary power of feeding, ruling, and governing the flock.

2. That the Roman Pontiff is therefore *Episcopus episcoporum*, and has for his diocese—the world.

3. That otherwise there would be lacking to the universal Church what is required in every particular Church to constitute and preserve its unity. Without an Universal Bishop there could not be an Universal Church.

4. That the universal episcopate of the Roman Pontiff does not exclude, but supposes particular episcopates. He does not govern the Church by Bishops, as by his administrators and vicars. He constitutes them *true princes of the Church*, with ordinary power over their flocks or dioceses, although subject to him as to its exercise.

5. In this sense, as if he were the only real Bishop, and all the others but his deputies, St. Gregory the Great refused for himself the title of *Œcumenical* or *Universal Bishop*—not that it did not really and of right belong to him, or that he did not exercise the powers which it, in the sense I have stated, implied. There was also another reason of prudence, from its assumption and abuse by the Patriarch of Constantinople, which induced him, in his humility, to adopt in its stead the title, which his successors still bear, of *Servus servorum Dei*—Servant of the servants of God. 'He that is the leader among you, let him become as he that serveth.' The words of the saint in his humility are but the converse of the thesis of the doctor. Servant of the servants of God is the counterpart and the equivalent of Prince of the princes of the Lord.

6. Hence, as the Apostles were equal to Peter in his

apostolate, but subject to him in his primacy, so are the Bishops of the Catholic Church equal to the Roman Pontiff in their episcopate, but subject to him in his supreme pontificate. The episcopate is one in origin and nature and identity, but it is not one in extension of authority and jurisdiction. The episcopal order and character exists, after the manner of a whole, in each; but it exists in the Supreme Pontiff as in its origin and root and matrix.

The tract-writers therefore are correct when they state our doctrine as that 1. the Catholic world is his diocese, and 2. that he is spiritually and ecclesiastically sole and absolute monarch.

They are wrong 1. when they state that, from the date of the Vatican Council, he is 'to be' so. He has been so since the day of Pentecost; and this necessarily, as is shown in my Letter, from the very nature of the constitution of the Church.

They are wrong 2. when they say that this reduces the Bishops to being but his 'commissioned agents,' and that the government of the Church becomes in his hands an *autocracy*. There is a difference between an autocracy and an absolute monarchy.

It is somewhat disingenuous to refer in a foot-note to the Council's quotation from St. Gregory, as a passage cited 'with a curious perversion of its scope.' They do not venture to place the passage before their readers. I place it before mine, and leave them to judge. It is as follows: 'My honour is the honour of the universal Church. My honour is the solid vigour of my brethren. Then am I truly honoured, when the honour due to each is not denied.'

In a word, be it remembered that the Council did not *make the Holy Father infallible*. To do so would have been an act beyond their power; to declare to all men, in words that no man might mistake, a Pentecostal truth was within their power, and became their office.

II. The tract-writers go on to say:

That the words italicised by them in the clause of the definition which declares, 'Therefore such definitions by the Roman Pontiff are of themselves, *and not in virtue of the consent of the Church*, irreformable,' were put in, almost at the last moment, by the Ultramontane majority, expressly in order to deal a heavier blow at the minority, who had asked 'that the consent of the Church should be laid down as a requisite condition of doctrinal definitions.' 'The decree,' continue the tract-writers, 'therefore explicitly denies that the Church (*i.e.* the Roman Catholic Church as a whole) contributes anything to the force of a Papal decree thus delivered. All is made to rest on the Pope's sole authority.'

The Catholic Faith touching on the points here in question is as follows:

1. That a General Council is a body, consisting of head and members—representative of the Church.

2. That a Council apart from and in opposition to the Supreme Pontiff would not be a General Council, inasmuch as it would be—not a body, but a headless trunk.

3. That therefore a large dissentient majority would not prevent the minority, in union with the Roman Pontiff, being a General Council, there being still head

and members, and therefore—a body. A General Council, in its nature and notion, follows that of the Church, of which it is representative. But the Church consists of the Supreme Pontiff and those in communion with, and subject to, him; and no majority of dissentients affects his and their being the Church, and possessing infallibility of belief and teaching. Therefore also no majority of dissentients in a Council affects the infallibility of the belief and teaching of the Supreme Pontiff and the minority in concord with him.

4. That when the Supreme Pontiff promulgates to the whole Church a definition in matters of faith and morals, even if he does so of his own accord, and without consulting the Bishops, yet he does so as in union with them, and not as severed from, and in opposition to them. There can be no severance in such wise as that he should be on one side, and the whole of his subjects on the other. This would be a severance of head and members, a decapitation, and so destruction of the Mystical Body, the indefectibility of whose existence is guaranteed by the promises of Christ.

5. That when the Supreme Pontiff and the Bishops in a General Council unite in a definition, that definition is the definition of the whole body, head and members, existing together in one perfect unity.

6. That therefore the Bishops, defining in union with him, are thus infallible; that apart from him they are not *actively* infallible; and that in severance from, and opposition to him they are schismatic and heretical.

In answer, therefore, to the objectors I remark:

1. That it is beside the question, as in no way affect-

ing the infallibility of the definition, whether this clause was 'put in, almost at the last moment, by the Ultramontane majority,' or not. It is not the method of arriving at the definition that is infallible; it is the definition itself. Had the insertion of the clause been the result of intrigue, it still remains that it *was* inserted; and it is the fact of its existence in the definition, confirmed by the Supreme Pontiff, which gives it infallibility.

To bring this truth into clearer light and sharper outline, I put an extreme case. Suppose, among the papers of a deceased Pontiff is found a note of authorities and the train of reasoning which led him to the theological conclusion which he embodied in a definition; and that all those authorities are transparently false, and all his syllogisms fallacious and unsound; it in no way affects the infallibility of the definition. Talent and science do not avail to give infallibility to a statement; and folly and ignorance in the individual do not detract from the infallibility of his definition as Supreme Pontiff. The principle of infallibility is the assistance of God the Holy Ghost informing the Mystical Body, as the Spirit of Truth, and guaranteed to its head to formulate and utter its belief.

I have put, I say, an extreme case, and one which cannot occur, since even the Pontiff's preparation of any dogma is under the special providence and direction of the Holy Ghost; but supposing it possible, it would not affect our thesis, which is—the infallibility of the definition itself.

The ordinary method of the Pontiffs in arriving at the theological conclusions which are to form the subject-matter of definitions, is to search the *loci theologici* or sources of theological doctrine, such as the Sacred Scriptures, the records of Councils, the works of theologians and canonists, and the like; to consult men learned in theological science; to take the opinions of the Bishops, either with or without calling them into council; and, doubtless, in any and all of those methods he has the aid and assistance of God the Holy Ghost, but neither of those methods is necessary. The question is, does he define? and the truth is, when he defines, he does so by the assistance of the Spirit of Truth, and so—infallibly.

A Council has its advantages as a method of arriving at his conclusion; and when those advantages counterbalance the necessary difficulties and drawbacks, he calls a Council. It is, moreover, a striking spectacle before the eyes of the world, and so adds an *extrinsic* authority to the definition: but *intrinsic* authority, and any real infallibility which the definition would otherwise lack, it does not and cannot give.

2. The statement that the insertion of the clause referred to was 'expressly in order to deal a heavier blow at the minority, who had asked that the consent of the Church should be laid down as a requisite condition of doctrinal definitions,' may or may not be true, according as it is understood. If it means that it was 'expressly in order to deal a heavier blow' at Gallicanism and Febronianism, which hold that acceptation by the faithful throughout the world, instead of definition or confirmation by the Supreme Pontiff, gives infallibility, then I agree with the objectors.

3. Their notion that the 'decree explicitly denies

that the Church contributes anything to the force of a Papal decree,' is false, in the sense and for the reasons I have stated.

III. With the assertion of the tract-writers, that 'no one who knows what he does can join the Roman Catholic Church unless he believes this dogma (of the Papal Infallibility); that to become a Roman Catholic on any other terms is now impossible; that to continue a Roman Catholic without real inward assent . . . . is to remain in the Roman Church under false pretences, to forfeit the Sacraments, to incur the penalties of heresy . . . . and ultimately to incur the perdition of the soul;'—with this I entirely and cordially agree. It is excellently stated, and it is true.

IV. The tract-writers tell us that they might 'dwell on the notorious fact, that up to July 1870 many voices which spoke in tones of authoritative confidence, from high places in the Roman Catholic hierarchy, had declared that this doctrine of Papal Infallibility was not, and could not become an article of the Catholic Faith. Not only had the once-powerful school of Gallican divines emphatically repudiated it; not only had Roman Catholic Bishops and clergy in Ireland, not very many years back, put on formal record their denial of it; not only had such an approved manual as Keenan's *Controversial Catechism* declared it to be "no article of Catholic belief," and affirmed that no Papal decision could bind under pain of heresy, unless received and prescribed by the teaching body, the Bishops of the Church; but many European Bishops had in recent times distinctly denied it to be part of Catholic doctrine; and American Bishops, just before the Council and during the Council, had expressed their conviction that it was out of harmony with Scripture and tradition, and that it contradicted the history of the Church as a teaching power.'

Assuming the facts, I observe three things:

1. That there is a distinction between authority and voices which speak 'in tones of authoritative confidence.'

2. That I have never understood that Gallican divines, Irish, European, and American Bishops, or even Dr. Keenan, were infallible.

3. That if their sentiments were as the objectors state, then it abundantly proves the opportuneness and necessity of the Vatican decree.

V. The tract-writers next bring forward a long list of pronouncements by Pontiffs in the past, as to various matters of faith and morals, which they assume to be false, and by their falsehood to disprove the Infallibility of the Vicars of Christ.

Each of these has its well-known and sufficient explanation in the Schools; and the solution of such 'difficulties,' as they are technically called, belongs to the 'Schools.' Hence it does seem to me rather incongruous to introduce them in a popular tract, intended, according to the express statement of its writers, for 'readers who may not have time for deeper investigation.'

Such an array has a certain show of learning which panders to the vanity of the ignorant and superficial reader; and in the adhesion of such the objectors will doubtless have their reward. But to gain a point in controversy by placing theological puzzles before the British public is—I speak with restraint—sharp practice.

One could easily follow suit with a better catena of authorities from the Fathers against the Divinity of our Blessed Lord. Each of these has, as I say, its well-known and sufficient explanation in the Schools, as they fall into the same category with the 'difficulties' quoted by the objectors against the Infallibility of the Holy Father. But to set forth such arguments in a popular tract would be, on my part, a diabolical use, or rather abuse, of knowledge.

VI. We have next 'the case of the unfortunate Pope Honorius.' The case is so well known, that I restrict myself to the following remarks:

1. What Honorius wrote was perfectly orthodox, in the sense in which he wrote it.

2. Even had it been otherwise, his letter was certainly not a dogmatic definition, as he himself expressly declares; and therefore, even had it been heterodox, it would have afforded no argument against the doctrine of the Pontifical Infallibility.

3. The anxiety of Sergius to have the Supreme Pontiff on his side shows the position held by the Holy See, and the belief of that day as to the necessity of being in union and concord with it.

4. The manner in which Sergius endeavoured to deceive and hoodwink Honorius proves his own conviction of the personal orthodoxy of that Pontiff.

5. The Pontifical and Conciliar censures of Honorius come to this—that they condemned him precisely for not exercising his gift of Infallibility, for negligence

in his Pontifical duty, for too great credulity in believing the protestations and explanations of Sergius, and for his 'economical silence,' whereby he permitted the Faith to be endangered through the machinations of that wily heretic.

6. Assuming the genuineness of the acts of the Council, which classed him among heretics, it is to be remembered that the word *heretic* was not always used then in the strict technical sense of the present day, to signify one who denied a revealed truth proposed for universal belief by the proper authority, but was applied also to those who, by negligence, criminous silence, or otherwise, had aided or abetted or permitted such denial.

7. I do not dispute the genuineness of the acts; but I do object to their being adduced as of undoubted authority. The very fact of a large number of the learned maintaining their spuriousness, and asserting the interpolation by the Greeks of the condemnation of Honorius is sufficient to take the genuineness of the present text out of the region of *certainty*, and leave, at the most, but the maximum of *probability* in its favour.

VII. The tract-writers next advert to the cases of Popes Vigilius and Liberius, and allow that 'the case of Pope Vigilius is not, properly speaking, relevant to the present question;' that 'he was not defining in the sense of the Vatican decree;' that the case of Pope Liberius cannot be 'fairly described as presenting a fatal difficulty to Roman Catholics, if the decree be strictly construed. Liberius was not, in the sense of the Vatican Council, speaking *ex cathedra.*'

These admissions serve to give a graceful appearance of candour to the tract. This is very cleverly done.

VIII. But what is the almost intuitive judgment of the ordinary mind? Those three are all that can be impeached out of more than two hundred and fifty Pontiffs, and the case against every one of those three breaks down miserably!

And yet we next hear that 'if his Holiness (Pius IX.) had possessed any real knowledge of ancient Church history, he could not have committed himself to a statement so conspicuously unhistorical,—in plain terms, so utterly false,' as that he, in proclaiming the dogma of Infallibility, was but 'adhering to a tradition as old as the Faith.'

1. Now, of course, we not only admit but assert that the *fact* of the orthodoxy of all the Pontiffs would not prove the dogma of their infallibility; but I do maintain that that fact suggests a *prima facie* probability, an *a priori* likelihood of the truth of the doctrine to every reasonable mind. Does there occur in all history another fact of the same kind?

2. I reiterate our doctrine, that the infallibility of a Pontifical definition does not depend upon the reigning Pontiff's possession of 'any real knowledge of ancient Church history,' but simply and solely upon the assistance of God the Holy Ghost, guaranteed to him in his exercise of his function of Chief Pastor, in feeding with divine doctrine the entire flock of God.

Our Anglican friends seem penetrated with the notion of 'justification by scholarship alone.'

IX. Another matter of history, and I have done.

The tract-writers profess great zeal for the purity of history, and rate us roundly for believing and teaching doctrines in defiance of historical facts.

They have given us a little bit of contemporary history. Let us look at it.

They say—'One word in conclusion: according to an epigrammatic sentence, ascribed to a very eminent Anglo-Roman prelate, a conspicuous promoter of the Vatican Council, and a Papalist of the extremest type, the dogma of Papal Infallibility, when defined by the Pope in the Council, "triumphed over history."'

This passage seems to point to the Archbishop of Westminster. His Grace at any rate satisfies the outline, and might stand for the picture.

That he ever said those words, or gave utterance to any idea which might be legitimately expressed by those words, I know to be untrue, for I have ascertained it. But suppose this statement goes uncontradicted, and that it is copied by other writers, and by the process of repetition acquires a wide circulation, and a few generations pass away, and all have gone hence who could of their own knowledge have given it denial, and then in the far future some one argues *a priori* thus: 'This epigrammatic sentence contains a folly which could never possibly have been uttered by any Catholic in his senses, and certainly not by the Archbishop to whom it is imputed;' that man will be accused and convicted of arguing in contradiction and defiance of historical facts. The learning and truthfulness, and opportunities of information of the tract-writers, as well as the number of other writers who have taken the statement from them at second hand, will be adduced as irrefragable proof of its historical truth!*

Such is the fate of history, even at the hands of historical purists.

The tract-writers may excuse themselves by saying that they have only given the 'epigrammatic sentence' as *ascribed* to the prelate in question. If so, they have made their case worse. They have left an impression on the minds of their readers, and, on their own showing, an *injurious* impression, by the retailing of a story which they themselves have only on hearsay.

But more than this: not only have they contributed towards identifying his name in the minds of their co-religionists with an inconceivable folly; but Catholics who hear the saying unquestioningly ascribed to one whose ecclesiastical position, whose personal character, and whose well-weighed and measured utterance gives authority and value to his words, may be led to adopt the idea, and make it their own, and disseminate it,

---

* Since writing the above my anticipations have been confirmed. I have by chance come across a sermon, just published, and preached a few weeks ago by the Rev. W. H. Cleaver, of St. Mary Magdalene's, Paddington, in which I find a passage which circulates this slander. It does not ascribe the saying to the Archbishop of Westminster. It does more; it quotes it, as if it were a matter of course and everyday dictum amongst Catholics. Mr. Cleaver says: 'Does history tell us of Pontiffs anathematised by their successors, anathematised by Councils? Yes; but then it is maintained to be the chiefest, the most conspicuous glory of this latest addition to the faith of Pentecost, that it is a *triumph over history*.' Four pages farther on he reiterates the phrase.

This sermon, along with passages full of bitter animosity against the Catholic Church, contains others of much beauty. May its author, before he dies, obtain the light of Divine faith, and become a loyal subject of him, a passage from whose protestant sermons he has, with a grim pleasantry, placed, by way of motto, on his title-page!

xviii

—that the Vatican definition 'triumphed over history.'

The names which the initials signed by the tract-writers represent — and 'H. P. L.' and 'W. B.' when found in conjunction, vouching for a tract like this, can signify but two persons in the Church of England—are revered by their party, by those who agree with them within that Church; but the name of the prelate into whose mouth they have put words which were never his, is revered beyond the limits of the British Empire, and his words carry weight throughout the world.

Thus have the individuals who accuse a General Council, headed by the Vicar of Christ, of having formulated and issued a statement 'conspicuously unhistorical' and 'utterly false,' themselves, and that in the very document of their accusation, propagated a statement which is at variance with fact.

So much for historical accuracy, and the value of even contemporary history by way of evidence.

What the Archbishop of Westminster has really said, may be found in the fourth chapter of his Pastoral Letter to his Clergy, entitled 'The Vatican Council, and its Definitions.' Among other things he there says as follows:

'Is there any tribunal of appeal in matters of history? or is there no ultimate judge? Is history a road where no one can err? or is it a wilderness in which we must wander without guide or path? Are we all left to private judgment alone? If any one say that there is no judge but right reason or common sense, he is only reproducing in history what Luther applied to the Bible. This theory may be intellectually and morally possible to those who are not Catholics. In Catholics such a theory is simple heresy. That there is an ultimate judge in such matters of history as affect the truths of revelation, is a dogma of faith.'

Again: 'I would ask, Is it scientific or passionate to reject the cumulus of evidence surrounding the line of two hundred and fifty-six Pontiffs, because one case may be found which is doubtful? doubtful, too, be it remembered, only on the theory that history is a wilderness without guide or path; in no way doubtful to those who, as a dogma of faith, believe that the revelation of faith was anterior to its history and is independent of it, being divinely secured by the presence and assistance of Him who gave it. And this is a sufficient answer to the case of Honorius, which of all controversies is the most useless, barren, and irrelevant.'

Again: 'Whensoever any doctrine is contained in the divine tradition of the Church, all difficulties from human history are excluded, as Tertullian lays down, by prescription. The only source of revealed truth is God, the only channel of His revelation is the Church. No human history can declare what is contained in that revelation. The Church alone can determine its limits, and therefore its contents. . . . The city seated on a hill cannot be hid, and *is its own evidence, anterior* to its *history*, and *independent* of it. Its history is to be learned of itself. It is not therefore by criticisms on past history, but by acts of faith in the living voice of the Church at this hour, that we can know the faith.'

Again, examining the relations of history to faith, His Grace continues: 'The objection from history has been stated in these words: There are grave difficulties, from the words and acts of the Fathers of the Church, from the genuine documents of history, and from the doctrine of the Church itself, which must be altogether solved, before the doctrine of the infallibility of the Roman Pontiff can be proposed to the faithful as a doctrine revealed by God. Are we to understand from this that the words and acts of the Fathers, and the documents of human history, constitute the Rule of Faith, or that the Rule of Faith depends upon them, and is either more or less certain as it agrees or disagrees with them? or, in other words, that the rule of faith is to be tested by history, not history by the rule of faith? If this be so, then they who so argue lay down as a theological principle, that the doctrinal authority of the Church, and therefore the certainty of dogma, depends, if not altogether, at least in part, on human history. From this it would follow, that when critical or scientific historians find, or suppose themselves to find, a difficulty in the writings of the Fathers or other human histories, the doctrines proposed by the Church as of divine revelation are to be called into doubt, unless such difficulties can be solved. The gravity of this objection is such, that the principle on which it rests is undoubtedly either a doctrine of faith or a heresy.'

Again: 'The revelation of the faith, and the institution of the Church, were both perfect and complete, not only before human histories existed, but even before the inspired Scriptures were written. The Church itself is the divine witness, teacher, and judge of the revelation intrusted to it. There exists no other; there is no tribunal to which appeal from the Church can lie;

there is no coördinate witness, teacher, or judge, who can revise, or criticise, or test the teaching of the Church.'

Again: 'The Church has indeed a history. Its course and its acts have been recorded by human hands. It has its annals, like the empire of Rome or of Britain. But its history is no more than its footprints in time, which record indeed, but cause nothing and create nothing.'

Again: 'The tradition of the Church may be historically treated; but between history and the tradition of the Church there is a clear distinction.... The tradition of the Church is not human in its origin, in its perpetuity, in its immutability. The matter of that tradition is divine. But history, excepting so far as it is contained in the tradition of the Church, is not divine but human, and human in its mutability, uncertainty, and corruption. The matter of it is human.'

Finally, and an 'epigrammatic sentence,' if you will. 'The visible Church itself is divine tradition.'

The Archbishop characterises the process of the opposition of the so-called 'scientific historians' to the Vatican decree as 'essentially heretical. It was an appeal from the traditional doctrine of the Catholic Church, delivered by its common and constant teaching, to history interpreted by themselves. It does not at all diminish the gravity of this act, to say that the appeal was not to mere human history, nor to history written by enemies, but to the acts of Councils, and to the documents of Ecclesiastical tradition. This makes the opposition more formal; for it amounts to an assumption that scientific history knows the mind of the Church, and is better able to interpret its acts, decrees, condemnations, and documents, either by superiority of scientific criticism, or by superiority of moral honesty, than the Church itself. But surely the Church best knows its own history, and the true sense of its own acts and documents. . . . It is passing strange if the Church should be incompetent to judge of these things, and the scientific historians alone competent. . . What is this but Lutheranism in history?'

Here then we have the real sentiments and words of the Archbishop of Westminster with regard to the relations between the Vatican definition and history.

Current anecdotes which 'ascribe' to him words antecedently improbable as his, and transparently absurd in themselves, ought, in fairness, at least to be interpreted in the sense of his undoubtedly uttered and *ex professo* words.

And do they contain one single statement, not only which is the equivalent of, but which could be colourably twisted into,—'the dogma of Papal Infallibility, when defined by the Pope in the Council, "triumphed over history"'?

The Vatican definition was indeed a blow to 'scientific' (*sic*) historianism, inasmuch as it rendered its practice both morally and logically impossible within the Church; and we have seen its natural issue in an exodus of such historians.

That it was a triumph over 'scientific history,' as these words are understood by those who profess to monopolise it, is abundantly, and to them but too painfully, manifest. Whether the Archbishop ever used words verbally equivalent to these, I do not know; but they represent his meaning in the passages I have quoted from his Pastoral.

That he ever did use the words imputed to him I deny; that it was disingenuous to ascribe them to him, and equally disingenuous in the tract-writers to retail such ascription, I affirm.

I owe my readers an apology for so lengthened a refutation. It is not the merits of the Tract, but the position of the tract-writers, which has called it forth.

The Tract is unworthy of them; but it is worthy of their cause.

W. H.

THE DIVINE TEACHER.

MY DEAR FRIEND,

You are searching after divine truth, and I congratulate you; for, sooner or later, you will most certainly find it; and when you have found it, you will have repose of mind, and peace of soul.

We have all of us a natural instinctive craving for the truth. It is what philosophers call the *proper object* of our intellects; that towards which they of their very nature tend, and by the possession of which they are perfected. Desire of certainty natural to man.

When they possess it, they have rest. This is that repose of mind which absolute certainty produces, and which it alone can produce. The maximum of probability will not give absolute repose of mind; for the very fact of a thing being but *probable* implies that its opposite has something to say for itself, and that something is a disturbing element, and prevents absolute undoubting repose of mind.

There are various degrees of certainty; but the lowest of them is not only higher than the greatest degree of probability, but it is in an entirely different order. A thing must cease to be merely very or most probable, before it can be in Degrees of certainty.

any sense certain; for probability implies some uncertainty. The maximum of probability implies the minimum of uncertainty, but still that minimum remains, and while it remains there is not absolute repose of mind.

I have said, 'There are various degrees of certainty;' and you may say, 'How can this be? How can certainty admit of degrees? A thing is either certain, or it is not. It cannot be more than certain.' I answer, 'As far as all the degrees exclude doubt, they are all equal; but inasmuch as the *motives* whereby the doubt is excluded may be greater or less, more in number or fewer, so the certainty may be said to be greater or less.'

For instance, I am absolutely certain, that is, I have no doubt whatever, that there is a country called Africa, although I have never seen it; my mind is perfectly at rest as to the fact; it never occurs to me to inquire as to its truth; and I should not give heed to the words of any one who denied it. The motive of my belief is,—because all men say so. That is my major premiss; my minor is, but all men cannot be deceived, or deceive; they cannot all be supposed to have combined in, or to be the victims of, one vast conspiracy to assert a falsehood; and my undoubting conclusion is, therefore, that there is a country called Africa. This is what is called *moral certainty*. This is the lowest kind of certainty, but still certainty. It excludes all doubt, and produces in my mind perfect repose.

<small>Moral certainty.</small>

Again, I am absolutely certain that the sun will rise to-morrow morning; and the motive of my certainty is,—the unfailing constancy of the laws of nature. This is what is called *physical*

<small>Physical certainty.</small>

certainty; and it is higher than the other, because the motive is greater.

But there is a higher certainty still. I am certain that twice two make four, and that the whole is greater than any of its parts. This is what is called *metaphysical certainty*, and it is the highest degree of natural certainty; and for this reason: such a thing as the universal deception, active or passive, of the world might be imagined; and there might be an interruption of the laws of nature, by their Lawgiver, the Creator of nature. Both are alike conceivable, being within the range of possibility. But such a thing as that twice two should make three or five, or that the whole should not be greater than its part, cannot be conceived as possible; it involves a contradiction. God Himself could not make it so. And this is no derogation from His omnipotence; for the impossible is not the object of, or within the sphere of, power.

<small>Metaphysical certainty.</small>

This, then, is what I mean by certainty,—which excludes all doubt, and begets an absolute repose of the mind. And now I affirm that I have a greater degree of certainty with regard to truths of the supernatural order, than I have with regard to those truths of the natural order. I have a degree of certainty higher than even the metaphysical—the certainty of divine faith. It excludes all doubt, and begets in my mind absolute repose; what St. Paul calls the 'joy and peace of believing.' I am more certain that there are Three distinct Divine Persons who are yet One God, that Mary was immaculately conceived, that her Son was the Eternal Word, and that the Holy Father is His Vicar and infallible, than I am that twice two make four.

<small>The certainty of divine faith higher than any of the three.</small>

But what is the reason? Why is it that I hold all this with absolute certainty, and you do not, although those truths are equally before us both, and we are equal as to our powers of understanding and reason, in forming judgments and arriving at conclusions?

The reason is not to be sought for in diversity of circumstances, or the difference of our antecedents, education, pursuits, temperament, or mental bias. These will account for much, but not for this.

<small>The light of faith.</small>

The reason is this; and I shall preface it by an illustration which will serve to explain it, and make my meaning clear:

I see the crucifix now standing before me on my table as I write; and that because it is visible in itself, and I have the power of vision in my eyes; but, supposing the room were in darkness, I should no longer see it, although it would remain in itself equally visible. and I should have the power of vision in my eyes as much as before. The presence of light, then, is necessary to vision, and its absence precludes it. In the same way, the reason why I, in common with all Catholics, believe those and kindred truths, while you, in common with all who are not Catholics, do not believe them, or hold them with absolute certainty to the exclusion of all doubt, is because we have, by the goodness of God, and apart from any merit of our own, a grace which is called the Light of Divine Faith, while you as yet do not have it. It is not our believing those truths which invests them with truth, or makes them to be true; and your disbelief of them equally does not divest them of that truth which they objectively possess. They are true apart from all affirmation or belief on the one hand, and from all denial or disbelief on the other.

Let me explain farther what I mean by this *light of faith*. God has given to His intelligent and rational creatures three great spiritual lights; I say *spiritual* or *intellectual*, to distinguish them from the material light which affects the bodily eye.

The first is the *light of intelligence* or *reason*, called otherwise the *light of nature*. It is by means of this light that I see clearly, for instance,— *The light of nature.* that twice two make four, or that the whole is greater than its part. Those are facts within the sphere and compass of my intelligence and reason, which, illuminated by this natural light, apprehends them and holds them with absolute certainty. But take another fact, which is asserted, that in God there are Three Persons, distinct and separate the one from the other, as to their personality, and yet identified with each other, and numerically one, as to their essence, substance, nature, power, will, operation, &c. To my reason, even with its natural light, this seems a paradox; and yet I believe it as firmly, and with as little doubt, as I do that twice two make four.

And why? By reason of a superadded, supernatural light, the *light of divine faith*—a grace, *The light of grace.* a quality bestowed by my Maker on my soul, illuminated and fortified by which it can apprehend and embrace undoubtingly truths, which by no power, or faculty, or force of nature I can even have knowledge of, much less embrace.

The third spiritual light bestowed by God is the *light of glory*, the correlative in the future of *The light of glory.* the light of grace in the present. By means of it we shall see God, behold Him intuitively, and no longer under veils. We shall seem Him as He is. Now we walk by faith, then we shall walk by sight. But this last and greatest light does not immediately concern us now; what I wish to speak of is the Light of Faith.

This gives absolute undoubting certainty. He who has it has perfect repose of mind, no disposition to inquire—he has no fear or suspicion of the possible truth of the opposite—and farther, no arguments will avail to persuade him of the truth of the opposite. Just as a clever mathematician might bring me a great number of seemingly irrefragable arguments, to persuade me that twice two make five, and I might fail to answer any one of them, or to see any answer, and yet I should remain firm in my conviction, fully and firmly persuaded in my mind of the truth that twice two make four, and retain my certainty unshaken and untouched; so also a clever controversialist might bring me an equal number of arguments against the truth of the Trinity, or the Immaculate Conception, or the Infallibility of the Holy Father, and, after all, I should remain in my certainty of belief as I was before.

You may put this easily into practice. You may ply a Catholic with argument after argument against some truth of the Catholic religion. You may be clever and learned, and he may be ignorant and a fool, and have not a word to say for himself; and yet you have not affected his belief. He is as certain as ever that his faith is right, and that your opinions are wrong.

But try the converse: will you expose a Protestant to the teaching of one of our priests, and not fear the issue? I suppose in both cases a subject whose intellectual vision is fixed steadily upon the truth, and whose sole desire is to possess it.

We have arrived, then, at this: 1. That the intellect tends of its nature towards the truth, and does not rest save in its possession. 2. That there are certain truths which it knows by the natural light with absolute certainty, and as to which it is at perfect rest, undisturbed by any doubt, without fear or suspicion of the opposite proving true, and not caring for, and never dreaming of inquiring farther. 3. That many men have equal, nay greater, certainty as to other truths which to reason appear at first sight paradoxical and contradictory. 4. That this is because they are not contrary to reason, but beyond its range and sphere, and therefore beyond the compass of its faculties and powers. 5. And that to have this knowledge and certainty, or, in other words, *belief*, the soul must have superadded to its natural endowments a supernatural quality which we have called the light of faith.

Those superrational facts are what we mean when we speak of mysteries. Two things are required and suffice to constitute a mystery: 1. that the fact itself cannot be ascertained, *that it is*, by any process of the reason; and 2. after we know that it is, that it cannot be fully and adequately understood by us, or comprehend, *what it is*, or *how it is*. Mysteries: what are they?

For instance, the doctrine of the Trinity is a *mystery*. We cannot, 1. by any process of the reason arrive at the fact, that there are three *separate* and *distinct* Divine Persons. There are trinities in nature, but none of the same kind as that which we affirm of God. Peter, James, and John are a trinity of distinct persons, and with an unity of nature,—their common humanity. But this is a *specific* unity.

Again, there is a trinity of powers with an unity of essence in the human soul. But this also is diverse from the Trinity of Persons in the Divine Unity of Essence or

Nature. That Essence or Nature which is in the Father is *identically* or *numerically*, and not merely *specifically*, the same Essence which is in the Son; and again, which is in the Holy Ghost. This we cannot know from reason, and we can know it only from revelation; and, moreover, after thus knowing it, we cannot, 2. understand or comprehend *how it is*. And yet we believe this mystery, enlightened and fortified by the light and strength of divine faith.

I have spoken of *revelation*. Now I do not mean in Likelihood of this Letter to prove to you the existence of a a revelation. divine revelation; we both agree as to the fact, although the grounds and motives of our agreement may differ, and consequently our acceptance of it, and attitude towards it. I shall only suggest a reason, which flows partly from what I have said, to show the antecedent probability, the *a priori* likelihood of a revelation. The God who made us, and whom we worship, is not a mere almighty force. He is a Spirit, and as such has an intellect and a will. Our intellect, which is formed after the pattern and model, the image and likeness of His, tends of its nature towards the *true*, and our will, in like manner, towards the *good*, and both are perfected by their possession of these. Reasoning from ourselves to Him, we know that His intellect and will so tend also; and we know moreover this, that there is, so to speak, a natural desire and inclination on the part of God to diffuse His goodness and truth outside Himself. He has diffused His being by creation; and to those creatures who are capable of its reception, that is, to the intelligent and rational, He desires to impart His truth and goodness. We see a shadow of this in ourselves, and from that we reason with regard to Him. A good man strives, as it were instinctively, to diffuse his goodness by making others good; and one who has acquired or is in possession of a truth, longs and strives to impart it to others, and that in proportion as he realises its truth, or in proportion as it becomes subjectively true to him. Or, to put it otherwise,—in God all things are one, save only where there is opposition of substantial relations, that is, save only the Three Divine Persons, who are personally and individually distinct the one from the other. Hence in God His truth and His goodness are not distinct from His being or essence, but identified and one therewith. In strictness, we do not say, God *has* truth and God *has* goodness, but God *is* Truth and God *is* Goodness. But goodness and truth are diffusive of themselves, as we have seen. And as God has diffused His being by creation, that is, by bestowing being, so also we should expect Him to diffuse His goodness and His truth to such of the beings whom He has created, who are capable of its reception. Such beings are His intelligent and rational creatures, angels and human souls, who both alike possess intellects and wills, which tend respectively towards truth and goodness as their proper objects, by the possession of which they are perfected.

Looking, then. to the Creator on the one hand, and beholding His tendency to bestow, and looking to His intelligent and rational creatures on the other, and beholding their capacity to receive, and the necessity of such reception, in order to their perfection, we anticipate that the two tendencies—the one, so to speak, downwards, and the other upwards—will terminate and meet in a revelation of divine truth. We have thus an antecedent probability and *a priori* likelihood of a revelation.

In the fact of a revelation, you and I concur, as **well**

as in the farther fact, that that revelation was made through Jesus Christ. We alike accept the words of the Evangelist—'No man hath seen God at any time; the only-begotten Son, who is in the bosom of the Father, He hath declared Him;' and those other words of the Apostle :—'What man knoweth the things of a man, but the spirit of a man that is in him; so the things also that are of God no man knoweth, but the Spirit of God; now we have received the Spirit that is of God, that we may know the things that are given us from God.'

<small>Jesus Christ the revealer.</small>

These two passages of Holy Scripture bring us to the point. Supposing you had lived in Judea during the days of our Divine Lord's mortal sojourn on earth and among men, and you had heard from His own lips some truth entirely above and beyond your reason to ascertain or to comprehend—say, for instance, the doctrine of Transubstantiation, of His real, true, and substantial presence in the Blessed Sacrament—you would have believed Him, would you not?

You would have reasoned: This man is God Incarnate; He has divine authority, divine mission, and a divine message; when therefore He speaks, God speaks, my Maker speaks. This doctrine is a mystery; my reason does not help me to the knowledge of it; and after I have heard it, I cannot understand it. But because of the divine authority of Him who declares it to me, I *believe* it; I accept it joyfully, and embrace it undoubtingly. He, the Incarnate Wisdom, cannot be deceived, and He, the Incarnate Truth, cannot deceive; therefore, 'O Lord, I believe; help Thou mine unbelief.'

You would not, like the men of Capharnaum, when this mystery was proposed by Him to them, 'have gone back and walked no more with Him;' you would, like

Peter and the Apostles, when He asked them, 'Will ye also go away?' have answered, 'Lord, to whom shall we go? Thou hast the words of eternal life.'

In short, you would have accepted His words, and that in the sense in which He meant them, and explained Himself to mean them. You would not have criticised His teaching, or questioned it, or opposed to it your own opinions, or brought it to the bar of your own private judgment. You would not have argued, Is this probable or reasonable? or even, Is this likely? You would not have looked at the doctrine itself, on its own merits and intrinsic grounds of likelihood, but you would have looked simply at the authority of Him who proposed it to you.

Had you done otherwise; had you looked at the doctrine upon its own merits, at its antecedent probability, its *a priori* likelihood; at its reasonableness, or its evidence apart from His authority; had it commended itself to you, and had you then accepted it on these grounds, you would not have made *an act of faith*, you would not have submitted yourself to a Divine Teacher. You would have simply agreed with His sentiments, after having tried and judged them; you would have held that doctrine, not as an article of faith, but as a matter of *opinion*.

This leads us to consider wherein faith consists, what constitutes an act of faith. It is a submission of the reason to a divine, and therefore infallible, authority. It is not opinion, or agreement with another, for that argues a certain equality. In order to faith, there must be a superior and an inferior, a teacher and a taught. We agree, then, in this, that we should both have submitted ourselves entirely and unreservedly to the teaching of our Divine Lord, and accepted that

<small>What is faith?</small>

teaching simply because He was a divine, and therefore an infallible, teacher.

But now suppose farther, that He had said to us,— 'I must go away; I must ascend to My Father and your Father, to My God and your God; but I leave behind Me these men, and whoso heareth them, heareth Me, and whoso despiseth them, despiseth Me. As My Father sent Me, so send I them.' Why then, clearly, as He had clothed them with the self-same divine, and therefore infallible, authority wherewith He was Himself invested, their words would have come home to your mind with the same force, and laid on your conscience the same obligation as His did. and your submission of your reason to their authority, and your acceptance therefore of their doctrine, would have been equally an act of divine faith.

_{Jesus Christ's bestowal of divine authority on His Apostles.}

Now, you must read your Bible backwards if you do not allow that this was precisely what our Divine Lord did with regard to His Apostles. He gave to them His divine authority, His divine mission, and His divine message.

But observe, it was to the Apostles *as a whole*, as one body, not to them singly and as individuals. He had formed them into an *unity*, into *one family* and *one kingdom*, and had appointed over them, as such, one father and one sovereign.

_{As one body.}

Peter was their prince, and so their centre and bond of unity. Suppose, by an impossibility, any one of the Apostles had rebelled against, and separated himself from Peter: he would have simply fallen out of that one family and that one kingdom; he would have become thereby divested of all that divine authority which belonged to it, and become again merely James, or John, or Bartholomew, or Matthew, as

_{Under one head.}

the case might be. Their subordination to Peter, their father and prince, and their continuance in the unity of his family and kingdom, was the necessary condition of their apostolicity, and so of their divine authority.

Just as a wise master builder lays first the foundation before he builds the house, so did our Divine Lord lay the foundation of His Church on the rock of Peter before He built upon it that house of God. The supremacy of Peter was not an after-thought; it was necessary not merely to the well-being, but to the very existence of the Church, according to the divine idea.

The question is not as to what He might have done had He so pleased, or as to what it would have been well for Him to have done, but as to what He really *did*. Now, you know the words of His promise to Peter, that upon him He would build His Church, and that the gates of hell should not prevail against it. You observe His assertion of its oneness, and of the *indefectibility* of its existence; that the infernal powers of evil, much more the might of men, should never succeed in its overthrow, although both should be arrayed and combine in attempting it. Foundation of the Church in Peter. Its indefectibility, and his infallibility and plenitude of jurisdiction.

Again, you remember how He told His Apostles, before His Passion, that Satan had desired to sift them like wheat, but that He had prayed for Peter, that his faith should not fail, and that he, when he was converted, should confirm his brethren.

Again, you observe *them* in the plural, and *Peter* and *his* unfailing faith in the singular, as the root and support of theirs; and here you have the promise of his *infallibility;* for surely if Peter could, by any possibility, err in his teaching, it would not have been to the confirmation but to the destruction of his brethren.

Finally, you remember how, after His Resurrection, He gave to Peter the *plenitude of jurisdiction*, and constituted him pastor of both sheep and lambs, Apostles and disciples, clergy and laity, putting him in His own place as chief shepherd over the entire flock of God. Thus He completed the work of the great forty days between Easter and the Ascension, which work was the constitution, construction, and setting in order of that kingdom, not of this world, which He was to have upon the earth; that absolute monarchy in the supernatural order, by means of which He was to rule from sea to sea; to acquire the nations for His inheritance, and the kingdoms of the earth for His possession; to reign until He had put all enemies under His feet; to be King of kings and Lord of lords; to exercise sovereignty, empire, and dominion over the intellects and consciences and wills of men, which were all to be made subject to the obedience of faith.

Having done this, His work on earth was at an end, and He ascended from it into heaven.

But why was it, then, that His Apostles did not, *What was wanting in His Church at the date of His Ascension.* upon His Ascension, commence at once to fulfil their mission? Why did they not disperse at once, and go each his way to preach the Gospel? Why did not their sound go forth at once unto all the earth, and their words unto the ends of the world?

Mark me, had they done so, the desire of Satan would have been accomplished, and they would have been scattered like chaff before the whirlwind. In the first place, it would have been an act of disobedience to the divine command. Our Divine Lord had charged them to remain at Jerusalem till they were endued with power from on high. They were not to depart thence, but to 'wait there for the promise of the Father,' till after the lapse of ten days, till the fiftieth day from the Resurrection, till the Day of Pentecost, when they should be baptised with the Holy Ghost. Then, when the power of the Holy Ghost had come upon them, He foretold and promised that they should be 'witnesses unto Him in Jerusalem, and in all Judea and Samaria, and even to the uttermost parts of the earth.' Hence it was that, instead of dispersing from the Mount Olivet, they returned to Jerusalem, to the upper room, and there for ten days persevered with one mind in prayer with the women, and Mary the Mother of Jesus, and with His brethren.

But what was the reason for the divine command which prescribed this delay? It is apparent when we consider the idea of our Divine Lord in the constitution of His Church.

He formed it after the fashion of a living body, with head and members. He had collected those members, and given them a corporeal oneness by sub-ordinating them to, and setting over them, a head — Peter, their prince. *The mystical body.* The mystical body was perfect and complete in its external organisation when He left it behind Him on the top of Olivet.

But something more was wanting besides mere completeness of external organisation. If it was to be a living body, it must be informed and animated by a soul, and the Third Person of the Blessed Trinity, God the Holy Ghost, *The Holy Ghost, the soul of that body.* was to be that soul.

Take an illustration: when God formed the body of the first Adam of the clay of the earth, when He had moulded and fashioned every limb, and given it outward form and feature, and inward organisation, there it lay on the ground in all its symmetry and beauty, a masterpiece of divine wisdom and power. But had the work of God stopped short there, had He not breathed into the face of Adam the breath of life and caused him to become a living soul, that body would have been subject to the natural process of decomposition; it would, by a law of its own being, have been, in a brief space, resolved into its constituent elements; it would have gravitated back, by its own weight, into the dust from which it was taken. It was the bestowal of a soul upon it that gave it life, and that oneness which is the accompaniment and result of life.

In like manner, during the ten days of expectation, preparation, and prayer between the Ascension and Pentecost, there was contained within the upper room at Jerusalem the Mystical Body of Christ—the Catholic Church—complete as to its external organisation, with head and members; but until the descent of the Holy Ghost it lacked its internal principle of life, and so of corporeal oneness.

It was, as it were, soulless, and so lifeless; and therefore amenable to the law of decomposition, which sooner or later affects all bodies which are devoid of souls.

Mark me well; realise this fully and clearly; it is the foundation of the whole matter. The Church of Christ was, 1. constituted by Him after the manner of a living body; 2. oneness of being is a necessary property and essential note of a living body; 3. in order to this oneness of being there must be a twofold principle of unity, an intrinsic and an extrinsic, an inward and an outward; there must be one indwelling soul informing the whole body and all its parts, giving it life, and binding them together in the oneness of one corporeal

<small>The necessity of a soul in order to the life and oneness of the body; as well as a oneness of body in order to the indwelling of the soul.</small>

life; 4. finally, in order to this indwelling of the one life-giving soul there is required, as a necessary condition, the external unity of the parts, of the members one with another, and of all with their common head; if that external unity is interrupted, this indwelling ceases, the intrinsic principle of oneness is gone, and decomposition is the result.

Suppose, for instance, the head of a living body is severed from the trunk, the continued indwelling of the life-giving soul is an impossibility; the whole body, head and members alike, is dead.

Suppose, however, a hand or foot to be severed from the body, the body continues to live, inasmuch as those members, although necessary to its integrity, its symmetry, its beauty, and its well-being, are yet not essential to its existence as a body. But the severed member is no longer inhabited by the one soul; consequently it is destitute of life; it is a dead thing, subject to decomposition, and fit only for the grave.

To apply this to our case. Supposing, by an impossible hypothesis, a severance of the head from the members of the Mystical Body, a rupture between Peter and the Apostles, or between Peter's successor, the Roman Pontiff, and the whole of the Bishops, he teaching and prescribing one thing, and they with one voice asserting its contradictory; in that case, the Mystical Body would be destroyed, the continued indwelling of the Holy Ghost, as its soul, would have become an impossibility, the promises of Christ would have come to nought, the gates of hell would have prevailed, Christianity would have collapsed. That this should be, we know is impossible; and therefore I have called such a severance an impossible hypothesis.

But suppose a severance between certain members,

few or many, great or small, on the one hand,—and the head, and certain members adhering to that head, on the other; clearly the one life, the result of the indwelling of the one soul, cannot belong to both, and, as clearly, it cannot belong to the members which are headless. If, therefore, it remains at all, it must necessarily remain with the head, and those members still in union with that head. That it must remain in the Mystical Body is, as we have seen, necessary in order to the verification of the promises of Christ. The indefectibility of the Church is guaranteed by them; with them it stands or falls.

Now this is precisely the Catholic thesis. 1. Peter as the head, and those in union with, and subject to Peter as the members, constituted the Mystical Body of our Divine Lord—the Catholic Church *then;* and the successor of Peter, and those in union with, and subject to him, constitute that same Mystical Body— the Catholic Church *now.* 2. There can be no severance between head and **members**; for that Body ever liveth, and is not subject unto death, to which it would be liable were such severance possible. Members may become diseased, and either fall off by their own weight, or be cut off, in order to the well-being and health of the body, by the amputation of excommunication; but this in no way affects its life, although for a time it may mar its outward symmetry, its beauty, and the proportion of its parts, contract its dimensions and decrease its size, and even seem to affect the vigour of its energy, and partially paralyse its action. But as to the severed members, they have lost not merely health and beauty, power and action, but life itself; they are existing apart from the one life-giving soul; they are no longer living with its life—they are dead.

Our Divine Lord constituted His Church after the manner, not of a marble statue, but of a living body. Keep this ever in view. He reiterates and confirms this idea by another instance of external oneness being necessary, in order to the possession of the one internal principle of life. He takes an example from another, and a lower species of life, the vegetative life, the life of a vine: 'I am the Vine, you are the branches.' The vine and branches together form one whole. 'The branch cannot bear fruit of itself, unless it abide in the vine.' A vine may be pruned down to the ground; for the time it may have lost its outward symmetry and beauty, it covers a narrower area than before, but its health and vigour are in reality increased, even if, in appearance, checked or diminished. But as for the severed branches, they no longer live with their former life, with the one life of the vine, in the oneness of which they once existed —they are dead, subject to the law of decay, fit only for the burning.

The constitution of the Church re-presented to us under two ideas: that of a living vine, and that of a living body; both requiring external oneness, as a necessary condition to the continued possession of life.

This principle, then, runs through all organic life: external oneness is a necessary condition to participation in internal life.

It is otherwise with the marble statue of which I have spoken. An arm may be broken off, and the symmetry of the statue is spoiled, the perfection of its beauty is at an end. But the severed arm has not changed its nature; it is of precisely the same nature as it was before, and of the same nature as that of the statue from which it has been broken off; the whole was inorganic, it was not a living thing; and the destruction of external oneness operated no change in the nature of either of the separated parts.

I think, my dear friend, I may now fairly assume that we are agreed as to the fact, that our Divine Lord constituted a Church, and constructed it after the manner of a living body, living with an organic life, with an indwelling soul, and that—the Holy Ghost; as well as with an external unity of body, secured by the subordination of all the members to one visible head, and that head—Peter.

On this Body, contained within the upper chamber at Jerusalem on the day of Pentecost, the Holy Ghost descended, and in a threefold character. 1. As the *Spirit of Truth*. Jesus Christ, the Second Person of the Blessed Trinity, the Incarnate Word, had, during the days of His mortal sojourn, taught to those with whom He came immediately in contact, many things concerning the Triune God, His own Incarnation, the relation of the Creator to the creature, and the correlative obligations of the creature towards its Creator; to the multitudes He spoke in parables, to His Apostles He spoke plainly. But He told them that when He was gone away into heaven, and had sent the Holy Ghost to earth, He, the Holy Ghost, should guide them into all truth, and bring all things to their remembrance, whatsoever He had said unto them. This, then, was the first office of the Holy Ghost; as the Revealer to declare to the Apostles the whole revelation of God, whatsoever God willed should be known and believed on earth by man. He consolidated and sealed up the entire Gospel and revelation of God. It was the ultimate revelation; there would be no new revelation. All that we know and believe now, the entire cycle of Christian doctrine in all its circumference, was known and believed then, by the Apostles on the day of Pentecost, before the sun went down.

[Side notes: Descent of the Holy Ghost on the Mystical Body: 1. As the Spirit of Truth.]

2. But it was not sufficient merely to reveal. Much of that revelation was beyond the compass of man's natural faculties to apprehend and embrace. He had need of supernatural faculties—of a supernatural light, superadded to the natural light of reason, of that *light of faith* of which I have spoken; and so the Holy Ghost descended on the Mystical Body as the *Spirit of Light*.

<small>2. As the Spirit of Light.</small>

3. Farther, in consideration of their weakness, and the difficulty of the work set before them, there was need of another grace, the grace of divine, supernatural strength. Physical or moral courage, or the natural strength of an iron will, would not suffice to sustain them in the struggle on which they were about to enter. Already, in the hour of trial they had failed miserably. One Apostle had betrayed His Master and Redeemer; another had denied Him; all the rest, with one exception, had forsaken Him and fled to secure their own safety; and this even after, and just after, they had been made one flesh and blood with Him, through the Blessed Sacrament. Nay, even after the Resurrection, Thomas doubted. Were those, then, the men to proclaim to the world the Gospel of the Cross, that was to be to the Jews a stumbling-block, and to the Greeks foolishness? Hence the Holy Ghost descended on them as the *Spirit of Strength;* and thenceforward from that day we read no more of betrayal, or denial, or flight, or doubt. They rejoiced not only to endure hardness, and suffer persecution, but what was harder still—*contumeliam pati*—to 'suffer *shame* for the name of Christ,' whose Gospel they proclaimed before kings and rulers, before great men and small, testifying to it even with their blood. They, instucted, enlightened, and fortified by the Holy Ghost.

<small>3. As the Spirit of Strength.</small>

went out into the world, which lay in wickedness, in sensuality, and in that unbelief of a darkened understanding which sensuality begets; and the victory that overcame the world was their faith.

In a word, the Holy Ghost descended on the Mystical Body to bestow upon it—
1. The knowledge of the faith.
2. The grace, or light of faith.
3. And strength, to fight the good fight of faith.

It was henceforth 'full of faith and of the Holy Ghost.' It was a living thing, with an external corporeal oneness, and with an internal life, sentiment, understanding, and will; the oneness of all made manifest by the oneness of speech and action in which all resulted.

But now, let us turn away from Pentecost to the present day, from Jerusalem to London, and inquire and see where is the Mystical Body, this Church of Christ?

We are surrounded by bodies, each calling itself a Church, and the Church of Christ. 'Lo! here is Christ! and lo! He is there!' How, amidst this Babel of conflicting claims, are we to ascertain, and know with absolute certainty, to the exclusion of all reasonable doubt, which is the Church of Christ, which is His one Mystical Body, which is animated by the one soul, the one Holy Ghost?

Where is, and which is the Mystical Body of Christ now, in our days?

Well, in the first place, let us purify our intention, and direct our spiritual vision; let us cut ourselves adrift from all entanglements of prejudice, whether of antecedents, or circumstances, of education, or of the temporal consequences which the result of our inquiry may entail. Let us look simply at the one point, Where is, and which is the Church of Christ? He clearly had a Church, and one Church, on earth once; and He, as clearly, has that Church now, or the powers of evil have prevailed, and His promises have come to nought.

Secondly, let us put aside all merely human learning, all histories, and all books of controversy. But why? For this reason: were the Church to be discoverable and known only in this way, by means of long, learned, and laborious investigation, salvation would be for the few, and not for all. All men have not brains, or learning, or leisure for such an inquiry; nay, more than half the human race cannot even read. Faith, then, is not to be got from books. 'Faith cometh by hearing.' Yes, it must be by signs and notes which are apparent to all; to the poor as to the rich; to the illiterate and the rude, as well as to the clever and the learned; to the apple-woman at the street-corner, guileless of culture and learning, as well as to the king in his palace, and to the philosopher in his study. She has a soul to be saved as well as they; for her, the Incarnate Word laid down His Life, and shed His Blood, as much as for them; and she has, equally with them, a right to know where is the Divine Teacher who will guide her into all truth. *Salvation not 'by scholarship alone.' Notes or signs of the Church, the Mystical Body. The Divine Teacher must be easily discernible, and apparent to all.*

Now, there are two notes of the Church of God, which are amply sufficient for our purpose; the first is her *unity*, the second is her *universality*.

As to the unity of the Church of Christ, I have already spoken: I shall only add His own words, the words of His prayer to the Eternal Father: 'That they all may be one, as Thou, Father, art in Me, and I in Thee; that they may be one in Us, *that the world may know that Thou hast sent Me.*' There was to be a unity so wonderful as to be sufficient evidence to men of His own divine mission; and therefore, and much more, of the divine authority of those whom He had intrusted with the divine message. *1. Its unity.*

As to the *universality* of the Church of Christ, it was

to embrace 'all nations,' and to be co-extensive with the 'whole world.' Those two characteristics were undoubtedly stamped upon that Church which our Divine Lord left on earth; let us therefore see whether any body of Christians possesses them now. To begin with those outside the Catholic and Roman Church, let us take the Church of England. It is one of the largest and most important, socially, politically, and in point of learning. Is it one? Assuredly it is not so! High Church, Broad Church, Low Church, and with infinite subdivisions of those three great parties, each of which contradicts and opposes the other on the most vital questions, in newspapers and on platforms, in the halls of convocation, and before the courts of law. Whatever it possesses, it has certainly not the note of *unity*.

2. Its universality.

These notes applied to the Church of England as a representative of the Protestant bodies.

But has it *universality*? As clearly, as certainly, as undeniably, no! Its very name defines its boundaries, which are those—not of the world, but of England and her colonies. It is, at most, coextensive with the British empire, and flourishes only within range of British gunboats.

Destitute of those two notes of unity and universality, which were stamped on that Church which our Divine Lord left on earth, the Church of England is assuredly not identified with it; and if this is the case with regard to it, with still greater force does the argument avail against the smaller sects, which are at once its offspring and its rivals. We may, then, dismiss it and them from our minds in our inquiry.

But there is another Church, from which that Church of England separated itself three hundred years ago; and that Church claims now, as it claimed then, and as it claimed for fifteen

Applied to the Catholic and Roman Church.

hundred years before, to be the one and only Church of Christ—to possess all His divine authority, His divine mission, and His divine message; to be the one Divine Teacher, by whose teaching the words are verified, 'They shall be all taught of God,' and whose law obliges the conscience of the whole human race. To her, and to her alone, she declares His words apply: 'He that heareth you, heareth Me, and he that despiseth you, despiseth Me.'

And now let us put her to the test; let us apply to her those two notes of unity and universality, and see whether she can make good her claim on our obedience.

Is she one? Undoubtedly and undeniably she is. This is certain, on the testimony of friends and foes alike. Her children know her unity by daily experience; her enemies assert her oneness by their language concerning her, their attitude towards her, their treatment of her. They may deny loudly her divinity, and assert her emanation from the Spirit of Evil, but they cannot deny, even to themselves, her oneness; if they do deny it in words, they contradict their denial by their deeds. They treat her as a *person*, as a living body, with a oneness of nature, and sentiment, and thought, and will, and action. They may fear her, hate her, despise her, in turn; ridicule her pretensions, or oppose her progress; speak against her, write against her, enact laws against her, persecute and endeavour to extirpate her; but whatever they do, it is always done towards one living body, with one heart, and mind, and will. Here you have the unconscious testimony of enemies, of the world, and of the devil, to the living corporeal oneness of the Catholic and Roman Church.

So also as to her *universality*. She is the Church of

the World, the Church of the Human Race, the Teacher of the Nations; she knows no frontiers; she exists, lives, teaches, acts, in every land. This is also a patent fact, known to all men, to friends and foes alike, which no man can deny.

But how do you account for those two undeniable facts, the unity and the universality of the Catholic and Roman Church, save on her own thesis? They are obviously preternatural, and cannot be adequately accounted for on any merely natural hypothesis.

Men do not naturally agree. Human minds, since the fall of the human race, tend naturally towards divergence. Put one subject before six men, and you will not be surprised if you have six opinions. *Quot homines, tot sententiæ.* How, then, do you account for the marvellous, stupendous unity of the Catholic and Roman Church, regarding it simply as a philosophical phenomenon?

So also as to her property, and note of *universality*—repugnant as it is naturally to the innate spirit of nationalism — of national prejudices, antipathies, and jealousies. On our hypothesis there is no difficulty; on yours there is no answer.

Look at the difference, my dear friend, between you and me, when we say the same words of the Creed, 'I believe one Catholic Church.' You say, 'I believe *One.*' No, not at all; unfortunately not by any means one: High Church, Low Church, Broad Church, with their internecine warfare, and their endless subdivisions. '*Catholic.*' Alas! again No; unfortunately coexisting only with the British Empire, and fitly termed the Church of *England.*

I say, in my turn, 'I believe *One.*' Yes, perfectly peerlessly, indivisibly, unalterably one. '*Catholic.*' Yes, coextensive with the world, teaching men in every place of the whole earth, where men exist.

With us, every word rings out full, and clear, and true: 'I believe One Catholic Church.'

Can you, my friend, ever again utter those words till you have made your submission, and acquired a right to say them? Will there not rankle in your conscience, a lurking consciousness of an unreality and a lie?

But some doubt, or deny the oneness of belief and teaching of the Catholic and Roman Church. Let us put it to the test. Observe, I assert oneness of *belief* and *teaching*, not of *opinion*. From the very fact of a thing being an *opinion*, it is manifestly not absolutely certain, either by way of evidence, demonstration, or authority. Catholics are free as the wind, as to all m of mere opinion, to hold as they please, to affirm or deny, according as reasons are present to their minds, for or against. Her oneness tested. Freedom of mere opinion within the Church.

When an opinion is clothed with certainty, it thereupon ceases to be an opinion, and becomes a known truth.

If, for instance, I can prove to demonstration that one of two opinions is a necessary consequence of some article of the faith, or is ontologically connected therewith, or is implied by, included in, or flows therefrom, I have thereby established its certainty, and the certain falsehood of the opposite opinion, so far as contradictory of, or contrary thereto. Such a truth, so demonstrated, is said to be certain, by certainty of *theological deduction*. Theological deduction.

It would moreover be held by me with the certainty of *divine faith*, inasmuch as I saw the reasons for its being necessarily an integral part of the revelation of Pentecost.

But it would not come home to the intellects, and so would not press on the consciences, of those who did not see those reasons, as an article of faith; and they therefore would not be guilty, and could not be accused of *heresy*, who denied it.

If I denied it, I should thereby be *subjectively* a heretic, but not *objectively;* subjectively, because I had denied what I knew to be revealed; but *not objectively*, because it had never been proposed by authority for my belief. I should be guilty *in foro conscientiæ* of heresy, I should be in mortal sin; and were I to die in that state, should go to hell; but I could not be convicted *in foro externo* of heresy, or called a *heretic*.

<small>Heresy.</small>

In a word, such a truth would be what is called *definable*, that is, it might be, at some time, defined by the proper authority, inasmuch as it was, germinally or implicitly at least, a part of the deposit of faith, revealed to the Apostles on the day of Pentecost.

But until it was so defined, it would not be of *Catholic faith*, that is, it would not bind the consciences of *all men*, whether they saw the reasons or not; and its denial would not be *heresy*.

You see, then, that in order to *objective heresy*, or heresy in the strict sense, two things are required; first, that the truth denied should have been *revealed;* and secondly, that it should have been *proposed* by the proper authority to the whole world, as a revealed truth.

Farther, according to the Catholic thesis, two things are certain: 1. that no truth can be defined which has not been revealed; and, 2. that every truth which has been defined was revealed.

But this by the way; what I wish to make clear to you is, that in matters of *mere opinion* Catholics are absolutely and entirely free. To take a trenchant instance which occurs to me;—whether the Eternal Word would, or would not have been incarnate, had Adam not sinned. This is, at present, a matter of opinion; there are two great schools of theological thought at issue on the subject; and every Catholic is free to take either side.

Our test of unity is to be with regard to matters of faith,—of belief and teaching.

Let us select two statements, which are both matters of fundamental and vital importance to every human being, and which must necessarily be either two grand truths, or two gross delusions: 1. that our Divine Lord is really, truly, and substantially present in the Blessed Sacrament; 2. that there is absolution of sin in the Sacrament of Penance. Now let me go and ask a Protestant minister—and by that I mean a minister of any body, other than the Catholic and Roman Church—whether those two statements are true or false. I go first to a High Churchman. He says, with explanations and limitations perhaps, but still says,—both are true. So far good. I go to his brother minister in the next parish, who happens to be a Low Churchman, and put to him the same questions. He replies that the Real Presence is a fable and a delusion, and that Confession is the curse of society. He has no limitations to make, and no hesitation in giving me a direct, plain, clear, and undoubting answer to my questions. But what is my conclusion as to the authority of the Church of England, and its pressure on my conscience? Here I have two teachers of that religion, precisely equal, both of them, as to their au

A practical test of unity.

thority; and, if I am bound by their authority at all, I am bound by the authority of the one, as much as by the authority of the other. Both press upon my conscience, if with force at all, with exactly the same force.

I think we may put aside the Church of England as an authority and a teacher, and with it, we may also banish into space the lesser sects, the offspring of its decomposition.

I go next to a Catholic priest, and put my questions. I receive from him an unhesitating affirmative to both. He speaks of the matter evidently with as much certainty, and as little doubt, as if the question were,—whether twice two make four. Moreover, if I ask his next neighbour, I find him precisely of the same mind; and so throughout London, throughout England, throughout Europe, and throughout the world. So much for experiment. But when I look into myself, I find in my mind an intimate conviction, that not only shall I never find a priest, in communion with Rome, asserting the contradictory of those two statements, within hearing of or to the knowledge of the ecclesiastical authorities, and retaining the exercise of his ministry, unsuspended, but that such a being is an impossibility. In fact, I have a *moral certainty* of the unity and identity of the teaching of the whole Catholic and Roman priesthood, throughout the world, past, present, and to come.

To put it otherwise, the case is this: when I speak to a Protestant minister, I speak to a *man*, who unfolds to me *his sentiments*, which may commend themselves to me; or, by his cleverness, acuteness, subtlety, ingenuity, learning, or eloquence, he may persuade me of their truth. But, whether they are truths or not, they come before me as clothed simply with his indi-

<small>The attitude of an individual towards a Protestant minister, and a Catholic priest, respectively.</small>

vidual authority, or with their own evidence. When, on the contrary, I speak to a Catholic priest, I feel that I speak, not to a man who unfolds to me his private individual sentiments; but to one who is simply the representative of a power, and the exponent of a system. I may notice in him mediocrity of talent, and inferiority of education, and rusticity of manner; but I feel that I am speaking to, and listening to the Catholic Church in his person. I know that what he says, every Catholic priest in Christendom will say; I know that when he teaches me any doctrine of his faith, he has all the Priesthood, all the Episcopate of Christendom, and the Supreme Pontiff at their head, behind him. Their united weight is pressing upon my intellect and conscience. If there is authority anywhere, surely it is here.

But now as to the question of authority: where does it ultimately reside, whence does it flow?

Take, once more, the type of a living human body, under which the Church, the Mystical Body of Christ, is presented to us in the Sacred Scriptures. True, the life-giving soul exists, as a whole, not only throughout the whole body, but in each of its several parts. But, as to the *operation* of that soul, there are special organs through which it operates, and the principal organ is—the head. *The fountain and source of authority, of knowledge and law.*

In it the soul operates in order to *knowledge*, and again, in order to *will*, and it is the medium of *utterance*. It is by means of the organs of the head that we develop and communicate our knowledge, formulate, and express, and impose our will. It is the organ of *teaching* and of *law*.

What is true of the natural body is true also of the Mystical Body It has necessarily a head, otherwise it would be,—not a living and a perfect body, but a headless trunk, and therefore a lifeless corpse. If there is a head of the Mystical Body, it certainly was Peter while on earth; and it is, as certainly, the successor of Peter now, unless we suppose that his crucifixion was the decapitation of the Body of Christ.

Moreover, we have found that the Holy Ghost—bestowed on the day of Pentecost on the Mystical Body as its indwelling, life-giving soul—was both to abide with it all-days, and to guide it into all truth; in other words, was to be the principle, not only of its immortality, or indefectibility of existence, but of its infallibility of knowledge and utterance, of thought and language. As then He descended upon the body as a whole, for the life and well-being of the whole; so did He also descend upon the parts, or, as it were, the several organs, in order to their several operations; and on the head in particular, as the organ of utterance, the fountain and source of knowledge and of law. The Apostles were equal to Peter in their apostolate, but they were subject to him in his primacy; as the Bishops of the Church of God now are equal to Peter's successor in their episcopate, as one and all equally Bishops, but subject to him in his supreme pontificate. There can be but one father in one family, and one king in one kingdom; a body has but one head, and a vine but one root.

But what do we mean by the Infallibility of the Roman Pontiff? for I suspect that your difficulties spring mainly from not clearly apprehending what we believe and teach; and that what you reject and condemn, we should equally with you reject and condemn, and more energetically, and with heavier censures.

The Infallibility of the Roman Pontiff.

Now I remember, when in Rome, during the Vatican

Council, that there were three ideas, as to our doctrine on the Infallibility, prevalent in the Protestant mind.

1. That Infallibility was synonymous with *impeccability;* that we believed that, in virtue of it, the Holy Father could commit no sin; and so they said that the doctrine was in contradiction to the testimony of even Catholic historians, who allowed that the private lives of some of the Pontiffs in past ages had not been to edification. *Various misunderstandings of it.*

2. Others supposed, that by Infallibility we meant *omniscience;* that the Holy Father knew everything, and could tell men everything if he chose.

The wiser of this opinion said, Why, if he is infallible, does he not define everything in theology, philosophy, politics, science,—*omne scibile*—all the knowable? Why hide his light under a bushel? Why bury his talent in the ground, and expose it only at long and rare intervals? Philosophy, for instance, is the great subject of controversy; why not issue at once from the Propaganda press an infallible manual?

The less wise thought it to be a legitimate and necessary consequence of our doctrine, that the Holy Father could tell the winner of the Derby, or the issue of a boat-race, if he liked; and that it would be simply unamiable on his part, were he to conceal his prophetical knowledge. The faithful at any rate might have the advantage of knowing infallibly where to put their money. I have heard also the supposition that, given the Pope is infallible, and that you had lost some article of property, you had but to telegraph to the Vatican, and the Holy Father, if so disposed, could tell you where to find it. But those were, I admit, among the less wise.

3. A third class supposed that by Infallibility was

meant *omnipotence;* and a leading journal commenced an article on the usurpation of Rome by the Florentine troops with something like the following: 'The occupation of Rome by the Italian army is an emphatic commentary on the late monstrous dogma of the Papal Infallibility. If the Pope was, as he asserts, infallible, why did he permit the soldiers of Victor Emmanuel to enter Rome?'

This last argument would have told equally against the Divinity of our Lord, as denied by His crucifixion; and was, in fact, used on that day: 'He saved others, Himself He cannot save; if Thou be the Christ, the Son of God, come down from the cross.'

But, my dear friend, neither of the three is in any way our doctrine; and the very notion is to us the subject of merriment, and, I must add, of pity.

So far as the Infallibility of the Roman Pontiff is concerned, he may be, without prejudice to it,

<small>The Catholic and true doctrine of the Infallibility.</small> 1. a man of scandalous life; 2. without talents or learning; 3. penniless, powerless, and an exile. The infallibility of his definitions does not depend upon his holiness, his human science, or his earthly position, but simply upon the fact, that he is head of the Mystical Body of Jesus Christ, and as such has a special assistance of God the Holy Ghost, the Spirit of Truth, to guide him into all truth.

Just as the head is that organ by which is expressed the mind and will of the one soul which pervades and exists throughout the whole body; so also is the Roman Pontiff the head of the Mystical Body, the organ of the mind and will of the one Holy Ghost, who, after the manner of a soul, exists throughout and pervades that whole Body. Now what is there difficult in all this? Is there anything extraordinary, or hard to believe?

Our Protestant friends say that by asserting the Infallibility of the Holy Father, we are trenching on the divine prerogative, and attributing to fallible man a property which belongs to God alone.

But, if I am not mistaken, our friends themselves are as strong as we are in affirming the inspiration of the Sacred Scriptures. Now what is this but proclaiming the infallibility of Matthew, Mark, Luke, and John, Peter and Paul? And if their infallibility does not trench on the prerogatives of God, why should the Roman Pontiff's? *The doctrine of the Infallibility of the Roman Pontiff no more difficult than that of the Inspiration of the Sacred Writers.* And then remember, we claim less for him than for them; for them we claim *inspiration*, for him *infallible assistance*. Both are equally sure and solid foundations of absolute certainty; but the one denotes a higher mode of divine action than the other, and we reserve the term *inspiration* to denote that mode. Speaking with the looseness of colloquial language, we might say, that a definition of the Holy Father was *inspired*: speaking with technical accuracy, we should not say so; we should say that it was infallible through the assistance of God the Holy Ghost.

While on the subject of the Sacred Scriptures, let us look at the position of those who appeal to them as their rule of faith. In the first place, the great mass of such persons can trace the Bible no farther than the bookseller's. They have been taught in childhood that it is the Word of God; *The impossibility of the Sacred Scriptures being the Rule of Faith.* and the force of prejudice founded on that early association suffices for their belief. But is this a reasonable ground for an intelligent belief in its inspiration, and can any reasonable ground be found which does not also include the Infallibility of the Catholic Church?

The Bible is a *locus theologicus*, or source of theological doctrine; and it is the chief, but not the only one. It is not the Rule of Faith. Its history and its form alike render this impossible: numbers of Christian men and women lived, believed, and died years before a line of the New Testament was written, and yet they were full of faith, and perfectly instructed in the Christian doctrine. Even after it was written, multitudes had never heard of it, and multitudes more had never seen it. Some had seen parts, for it was written in parts, and the parts were preserved at places separated by long distance and infrequent communication. One epistle was in Rome, another at Corinth, a third at Colosse, a fourth at Thessalonica, a fifth at Philippi, and so on. Doubtless the several churches by degrees, and in process of time, exchanged their treasures; yet still all the time numbers of the faithful were living and dying, believing in, and practising their religion, without any Scripture or written rule of faith. It was not until the Council of Carthage, in the fourth century, that all the various parts of Holy Scripture were collected into one whole, their authenticity, genuineness, and canonicity established, and the volume stamped by the Church as inspired. The seal of the living Church of God is the ground of our rational belief in the inspiration of her sacred books. Farther, considering the nature of its contents, the scope of the several epistles, written to meet circumstances as they emerged, and requiring consequently on the part of their readers a knowledge of those circumstances in order to an intelligent understanding of the text; it is apparent that the very nature of the sacred writings precludes them from being a rule of faith, or being taken as a coherent and adequate system of theological doctrine.

Moreover, the difficulty of many passages, and the

controversies as to their meaning, manifest the necessity of an interpreter. The man of Ethiopia, the eunuch of great authority under Queen Candace, experienced this as he sat in his chariot, in the way that goeth down from Jerusalem to Gaza, and read Isaias the Prophet; and he allowed it to Philip the deacon, who asked him, 'Thinkest thou that thou understandest what thou readest?' and he said, '*How can I unless some man show me?*'

Farther, you remember how St. Peter himself points this out: when, speaking of the Epistles of St. Paul, he says that in them 'are certain things hard to be understood, which the unlearned and unstable wrest, as they do also the other Scriptures, to their own destruction.'

Our friends are, then, in a dilemma. Either, by their private interpretation of Scripture, they are putting themselves in peril of their damnation; or they assert their own learning and stability, and this is scarcely humility.

But do not mistake me: I have a great affection, and in a manner a reverence, for those Bible Christians, as they are called; and for this reason. True, they worship they know not what; it is an irrational worship,—it is, if you please, something akin to Fetish worship, or to the worship by the Ephesians of their goddess Diana, who fell down to them out of heaven from Jupiter; but with all those drawbacks, it is the nearest approach to an act of faith which is or can be made out of the Catholic and Roman Church. There is *a submission* of reason and will *to something divine, as divine.* Low-Church submission to the Bible, as the rule of faith.

They are hopelessly at sea as to *why* it is divine, and why it possesses a divine and so supreme authority over their consciences: and even in their worship there is a large alloy of private judgment; for what they submit to is, the Scriptures not simply as objectively true, but as subjectively true to them, that is, as interpreted by them. Yet still there is a submission to an authority, and so at least a shadow of an act of faith. They are irrational, but they are religious; they are puzzle-headed more than proud. They assert and act on the principle of Infallibility, although they are wrong as to its subject; transferring to an inanimate object that which is the property of a living Body—the Church of God, and its visible Head, the Roman Pontiff.

Now as to our High-Church friends, what is the ground of their faith? To what authority do they submit their reason? They answer—'To the Church.' But what Church? Certainly not the Catholic and Roman Church, for they lie under her excommunication. Certainly not the schismatic Greek Church; for even separated as it is from the Catholic Church, it will not ally itself with Protestant sects. What remains? The Church of England. But do they submit their reason to it, as to a divine and infallible authority? Read their organs, and the articles full of abuse and ridicule they contain against the ecclesiastical authorities of that Church, and the accusations of heresy they bring against its heads, including the Archbishop of Canterbury, and say whether they submit their reason to its teaching and authority, to its mind and will.

High-Church submission to 'the Church.' But what Church? Their notion of a Church.

Certainly they are right in this, that given the divine truth of the doctrines they hold in common with the Catholic and Roman Church, their archbishop is a heretic. But does this help their position? Nay, what does it entail upon them as a necessary consequence? It is an acknowledged principle, that those who are

Whether in submission, or in resistance to their authorities, they are equally heretics, on their own showing.

in communion with heretics are partakers thereby in their sins, they are heretics also. But they accuse their archbishop and the majority of his colleagues of heresy, and yet they are in communion with them; therefore they are themselves heretics on their own showing. They must take their choice of one or other term of the dilemma. If their archbishop is right, they are necessarily heretics; if they are right, he is a heretic, and they, being in communion with him, share his heresy.

Now, can you imagine me, for instance, writing in the *Tablet* of the Archbishop of Westminster as they, week after week, write of their bishops? What would be the consequence in my case, if I did? You cannot doubt but that I should be immediately suspended. There would be an exercise of authority on the part of my ecclesiastical superior; and on my part, if I wished to remain in his communion, there would be a necessary act of submission. Impossibility of this attitude in the Catholic Church.

If, on the contrary, I persevered in my contumacy. I should be excommunicated; and if any of my brethren in the priesthood or of my people adhered to me, they would share my excommunication.

True, I might be in the right, and he in the wrong; and were I persuaded of this, I might appeal to him who is superior to both of us—to the Supreme Pontiff. He is the Bishop of my Archbishop as well as mine; and my Diocesan is as much subject to the jurisdiction and authority of the one Father of the One Family, the one King of the One Kingdom, as I am. And were the Holy Father to sustain my appeal, and decide that I was in the right, and my Archbishop in the wrong; he would submit to his superior, acknowledge his fault, and repair his error. In my appeal there would be no insubordination, and in his submission there would be no indignity.

But were he to resist the judgment of his superior, the Holy Father, his excommunication would follow in due course, and thereupon his subjects would renounce their allegiance to him. If they adhered to him, from personal affection, for worldly advantages, or from private judgment, they would simply share his excommunication, and be, like him, members severed from the one Living Body—branches broken from the one Mystic Vine.

Here you have authority in action; and submission its correlative.

Remember, I do not blame our High-Church friends, and far less do I accuse them, in their attitude towards the Church of England, of ecclesiastical insubordination, or want of submission to, and rebellion against, a divine authority; that is a sin which their circumstances render it impossible for them to commit. In order to insubordination and rebellion on the one hand, there must be authority on the other. The two are correlatives; where the first is wanting, the other cannot exist; where the first does exist, it gives character to the other. Now the Anglican bishops possess merely civil authority, as persons of high rank in the civil service; and disrespect or disobedience to them is simply a civil misdemeanour.

In a word, the authority must exist, in order not only to compel the act of submission, but to generate the spirit of submission.

But to what Church, then, do our High-Church friends submit their reason in order to an act of divine faith, productive of absolute certainty, and exclusive of the possibility of doubt? Evidently to neither of the three authorities, the Roman, the Greek, or the Anglican. To what then? 'To the primitive Church,' say some; that is, the Church during the first three centuries; others say, 'To the undivided Church,' or 'the Church before the separation of East and West, meaning thereby the Photian schism. Again our friends find themselves in a dilemma; they must say either that the Church was once infallible, or that it never was. If it never was, why should they submit their reason to it? To do so would be an abuse of God's greatest natural gift. If it once was infallible, how could it cease to be so and still exist?

The same reasons exist for its perpetual infallibility as for its indefectibility or perpetuity of existence; and those reasons may be all reduced to this—the perpetual indwelling of the Holy Ghost in the one Mystical Body of Jesus Christ, alike as the Lord the Lifegiver, and as the Spirit of Truth, who should guide it into all truth. 'There is one Body and one Spirit.' Two souls cannot inform one body, and two bodies cannot share one soul; and the one soul cannot reside in the two severed portions of a divided body; the law of life forbids all alike.

What is, then, this Church, to which they say they submit their reason, and which, they say, teaches them the divine truth? It is a phantom, a spectral Church, existing in the air, or at most on paper. It has never been realised and never seen. It is their own offspring, the creation of their own imagination; begotten, borne, and brought forth by the action of their own minds. Its sole unity is the unity of their own conception. It is supposed to be the logical result of a mental fusion of Roman, Greek, and Anglican—the latter being the formal principle. The process of excogitation is as follows:—the conceiver has before his mind Roman and Greek doctrine, practice, and discipline: he has also in his mind an outline of an ideal Church: from the Roman and Greek treasure-houses he selects a doctrine, or a practice, or a point of discipline which commends itself to him, and fits it in: and he continues the process until he has filled up the outline, and completed the mental picture. This ideal Church is that on which he grounds his faith; and that to whose authority he fancies himself to bow. Need I say that the shifting sand is a more solid foundation than a spectral vision; and that real submission to a phantom authority that exercises no real pressure—that has no power of coaction because none of resistance—is an impossibility?

Now what is all this but Protestantism in its most quintessential form; the principle of Protestantism in its most complete development; the practice of Protestantism carried to its greatest length? It is private judgment from beginning to end. The *Ego*—the individual High Churchman—is himself the supreme arbiter; his conception of what ought to be, the norm; and his judgment, the ultimate tribunal.

<small>The radical and quintessential Protestantism of High Churchism.</small>

The difference between a Catholic and a High Churchman comes to this: the Catholic is *taught by* his Church, the High Churchman tries to *teach his Church*. It is their own phrase: they say they are endeavouring to *catholicise* the Church of England! Galvanism may do much. It produces spasmodic action, and it has a ghastly look of life; but it cannot supply the place of the departed soul. It cannot produce life itself, and thought, and speech, and action. As in the case of our Low-Church friends, so also here, we find the principle of Infallibility implicitly asserted, and really acted on; although there is an error as to its subject. So true is it, that he who believes not in the Infallibility of the Vicar of Jesus Christ believes in his own.

If then, my dear friend, you have followed me thus far, you must now see with me the reasonableness and the necessity of the Infallibility of the Supreme Pontiff, if we are to be in possession of the Divine Truth, and in subjection to the Divine Law; that there may be a real act of submission of the reason to a divine, and so infallible, authority,—which submission is faith; and a real act of submission of the will to a divine and infallible law,—which submission is charity. 'If ye love Me, keep My commandments.'

Take two out of many rational arguments to prove this. 1. Suppose the Holy Father not to be infallible, but liable to err in his teaching on matters of faith and morals. As Father of the One Family, as Sovereign of the One Kingdom, humility and obedience alike necessitate our submission—as his children and his subjects—to his teaching and his laws. But if he, from whom there is no appeal, teaches error—and, if he is not infallible, that is a possibility—then we are led into error by the practice of those two virtues; and we should be saved from it only by acts of the opposite vices, by acts of pride and disobedience. 2. Again, if an individual Bishop, or an Archbishop, or a Patriarch teaches error, his erroneous teaching affects in this way only his diocese, his province, or his patriarchate. But if the Teacher of the World err in his doctrine, the whole human race is led into his error. 'The Son of Man, when He cometh,' will not 'find faith upon the earth.' Christianity will have collapsed, the promises

The logical necessity of the Infallibility of the Supreme Pontiff.

of Christ will have come to nought, 'the gates of hell' will have prevailed.

<small>The assertion that his Infallibility is contradicted by historical facts.</small> But, say our friends, 'The assertion of the Infallibility of the Holy Father is in the teeth of history, and you cannot contradict facts.' We deny this. We maintain that it is in accordance with history, and that historical facts go to prove it. Not that I am going now into history, or intend to prove it to you in that way. If you are to believe it at all, you will believe it from what I have already said. But I do wish to point out to you two or three radical errors underlying our friends' objections. 1. They are subordinating the science of <small>The mutual relations of history and dogma.</small> theology, the most perfect and the queen of all sciences, to history, which, with all its value, cannot, in any strict sense, be called a science. 2. History must, from its very nature, be always incomplete, from the loss of historical monuments, the untrustworthiness of witnesses and writers, the fragmentariness, onesidedness, and sometimes inaccuracy of their narratives; and from the lack of the light of the past, whereby to read the past. 3. They are transposing history and dogma from their relative positions of priority, in the order both of time and nature. The dogma of the Church came before her history; and therefore history is to be read in the light of dogma, and not dogma in the light of history. The dogma of the Church was perfect and complete in its entire circumference on the day of Pentecost; on that day the Church had as yet no history. The Church is her own evidence; she needs no other, and she can best tell her own history; for she is inspired by the Holy Ghost, and she cannot lie.

But, say our friends, 'The Living Voice of the Church, as uttered by her Visible Head, is in contradiction to her Tradition.' Again they mistake our doctrine, and fail to apprehend what we mean by the *tradition* of the Church. There is a twofold tradition—a living and a dead. By a *dead* tradition, I mean a statement to be handed on as it stands, without increase or diminution from one individual to another. Such a tradition, like every dead thing, is unalterable, save by way of decomposition and corruption, and towards this it tends by an almost inevitable law.

<small>Tradition twofold—a dead and a living. The living voice of the Church the utterance of her living tradition.</small>

Relate, for instance, a fact to a friend, who repeats it to a third person, and he to a fourth. Let this repetition proceed, and in proportion to the passing time and to the number of individuals who are the vehicles of transmission, the relation will lose its original form and perfection, until at last its original author would fail to recognise it as his own.

But in the case of an *idea* existing in our minds it is otherwise. Instead of alteration by way of decomposition and corruption, it alters by way of increase of unity and completeness. The intellect contemplates it as a whole, and in its parts; in their relation the one to the other, and to the whole; as well as in its relation to other ideas, whether by way of similarity or contrast. As a living thing, it increases till it has attained to its perfection and the limit of its growth. It generates other living ideas, fruitful and prolific as itself; and it possesses two properties of a living thing: the power of *assimilation*, whereby it incorporates, or assumes into its own unity whatever is homogeneous with itself; and the power of *rejection* or *expulsion*, whereby it throws off whatever is heterogeneous to itself, alien or inimical to its nature.

These processes of intellectual life, which belong to an idea, belong to that deposit of absolute truth which was implanted, in its completeness, in the one collective mind of the one moral person, or individual unity, of the Catholic Church on the day of Pentecost. That deposit, or body of theological truth, thus implanted after the manner of an idea, is a living thing, living with an intellectual life, energising after the manner of that life, and—in accordance with its laws—generating, assimilating, and rejecting, and thus perfecting itself, and gaining in unity and completeness, as the years pass by.

The tradition, therefore, of the Catholic faith is not its continued relation from individual to individual— from father to son, from generation to generation —but its continued existence in one individual mind throughout all generations of men, and from age to age.

The identity of knowledge and thought in the collective mind of the Mystical Body is as complete as the identity of the Mystical Body itself, as it existed, with the dimensions of its infancy, in the upper chamber on Pentecost, with the Mystical Body extended throughout the world at the present day.

Men who study physical science tell me, that there is not a single particle now in my body of the matter which existed in and composed it in the days of my childhood; and yet they allow, I am persuaded of, and no one doubts, my identity now with the child of those days. So, also, I know that there is no one now on earth who was in the upper chamber as a member of the Mystical Body on the day of Pentecost. And yet I am absolutely certain, without the shadow of a doubt, of the individual identity of the Catholic and Roman Church of the nineteenth century with the Church which then persevered in prayer with Mary, the Mother of Jesus.

But farther, an idea in the mind of man tends towards utterance; and utterance is necessary in order to its communication. It must be clothed in, and expressed by words. Now what is a word but an expressed idea? The spoken word is but the outward expression of the conceived idea. The word that issues from the lips, and the idea which exists in the mind, are in reality identified; and the one cannot be in conflict with, or in contradiction to, the other.

It follows, therefore, that the Living Voice of the moral person, or indivisible unity, of the Catholic Church, giving, as it does, but outward expression to the idea living and vitally energising within the one collective mind of that person, cannot save represent it, and that there can be no collision or divergence between the two.

Again, the indwelling of the Holy Ghost, the Spirit of Truth, in the Mystical Body, after the manner of a soul, as it pertains to the whole body as well as to its head; so does it bestow on the whole body, as well as on its head, infallibility of thought and utterance. And this is what theologians call the *passive* infallibility of the entire Catholic Church *as a whole*—as the entire Mystical Body; not on the members apart from their head: for they would constitute, not a living body, but a headless trunk; but as, along with their head, they form one body.

But to the head it belongs, as the organ of utterance, to formulate thought, and to express ideas in adequate language, and to reject, deny, and condemn all ideas, language, and formulas discordant with, and in opposition to, its own. In order to the fulfilment of this necessary function of the intellectual life of the Church, there exist the *active* infallibility of the Roman Pontiff, its visible head; and this infallibility extends to all matters of faith and morals, and to all things else which have any essential, organic, connection with either.

This is a popular explanation of what is called the doctrine of *Development;* or, as I prefer to call it, and was taught at Rome to call it, the *Explication* or unfolding of the Catholic doctrine. There is no extrinsic accretion to the faith of Pentecost, but a natural process of evolution, the necessary result of its existence as an idea in the one mind of the one Mystical Body, according to the laws of intellectual life.

<small>Development of Christian doctrine.</small>

But, in any case, say our friends, 'You ought not to deny our orders.'

I need scarcely encumber my Letter by any remarks upon the subject of 'Anglican orders,' as, if you have followed my argument, you will agree with me, that it has but little bearing on the real issue; it is a matter which may be interesting to antiquarians, but, as a practical question, it is valueless.

<small>The validity of Anglican orders.</small>

If the ministers of the Church of England have valid orders, and are really priests, their position is worse than we, who believe them to be amiable and cultured laymen, at present regard it. It would still remain that they are schismatics; and, in that case, they would simply be schismatic priests, instead of schismatic laymen. The guilt and danger of their position would be intensified. They talk of apostolic succession as if that would make them an integral part of the Catholic Church. What avails it that the dead branch was once part of the living and fruitful tree, or that the amputated limb was once part of a living man?

But, say they, 'Rome has given no definite utterance on the subject; she has never, in so many words, said that our orders are invalid; and therefore, even in regard of her, it remains an open question.' I answer, 'Suppose a man knocks you down, or at least pursues a consistent course of action utterly subversive of your position, and in direct contradiction to your sentiments and language, can you, with any show of reason, persevere in saying that he regards the matter in dispute between you as an open question, inasmuch as he has not in so many words denied your statement?' The idea is repugnant to the common sense of mankind.

But this is precisely the case with regard to the unvarying attitude and consistent action of Rome in respect of Anglican orders. For three centuries she has ignored them, and, by her practice, signified her judgment as to their utter invalidity. Hundreds of persons, once ministers of the Church of England, have made their submission to the Divine Teacher of the Nations. And what has been their uniform treatment at her hands? They have first been conditionally baptised, in order to render certain their reception of that sacrament; next unconditionally confirmed—thereby entirely ignoring the orders and ministerial acts of the Anglican prelates; and finally, if they have been found, after due trial, to have a vocation to the ecclesiastical state, they have been unconditionally ordained.

I think the attitude and deliberate judgment of

Rome as to Anglican orders is tolerably apparent. She believes them to be absolutely null and void.

Moreover, the fact that a man has been a Protestant minister is no sign whatever of his vocation to be a Catholic priest; any more than a woman having been in a Church-of-England 'sisterhood' is a sign of her vocation to the religious life. Hence it is no discredit to either, when, finding themselves to be simply lay persons, they betake themselves to the pursuits and amusements which become, and are lawful in that estate. To act on this principle is to share in what is called the 'deterioration of converts.' You see how absurd and unreasonable is the charge. Why should not laymen live like laymen?

'But,' say our Anglican friends, 'there has been no formal investigation of the validity of our orders on the part of Rome. And the Bishops who have ordained clerical converts from Anglicanism, have simply followed the practice which they found current in their communion, without taking pains to ascertain whether it was in conformity with historical facts and the necessary theological consequences of those facts, or not.'

You will observe that the objectors have actually played into my hands. This is precisely my case, and the foundation of my whole argument. Ours is not a paper Church, trammelled by visionary conditions; but a living reality. It is the Mystical Body of Christ, with an organic and intellectual life, the issue of the indwelling of the Holy Ghost as its Mystical Soul. He who guides it into all truth guarantees the rectitude of its action, as well as the unerring truth of its thought and language; and we can argue from its procedure or consistent action as well as from its uttered words, for both alike express its sentiments and judgment.

Our friends have never fully apprehended and adequately realised what is implied in the perpetual assistance of God the Holy Ghost; and that that, and that alone, and not intellectual ability, or critical acumen, or historical investigation, or learned research, is the principle of the Church's infallibility of thought and judgment, whether expressed by words or actions.

I do not believe what the Church teaches me *because* my reason tells me, upon investigation, that it is true, but simply *because she teaches me*. I know that when she speaks, her words express the mind and will of God the Holy Ghost; and that if I reject them, I resist Him; if I criticise them, I criticise Him; if I bring them to the bar of my private judgment, I judge my Maker.

So, also, when I see the action of the Church, I do not approve it because my knowledge tells me that it is in accordance with facts; I simply behold the finger of God, and recognise His action.

This is akin to the religious attitude of the creature in respect of the Providence of the Creator. God has given me a manifestation of His mind in His Revelation; and a manifestation of His will alike in His Law and in His Providence. If I rebel against what occurs to me in the Providence of God, it is a sin of the same order as that which I commit when I transgress His Law. It is not to the *mode of manifestation* in either case which I look: it is to the *will* itself, which both alike express and make

[margin: The Church's action as well as her language an index to her mind and will; in like manner as the Providence of God is equally with the law of God, a manifestation, or outward expression of the Divine Will.]

manifest. So, also, I know the mind and will of the Church of God from her action, as well as from her words; and if I criticise, or judge, or condemn her action, it is but another form of the same sin which I should commit, were I to disbelieve her teaching, or break her laws.

<small>Another Anglican dilemma.</small> You will see that our Anglican friends are here again in a dilemma. They claim some sort of an occult connection with the Catholic and Roman Church, and it is necessary to their position; but if their orders are really valid, then that Church has been for three hundred years practising a systematic course of sacrilege — for both Confirmation and Orders are Sacraments which can be conferred but once, and to reiterate them is a sacrilege. Either, then, the Catholic and Roman Church is not sacrilegious—and in that case 'Anglican orders' are invalid, and Anglican ministers are laymen; or they are really priests, in which case she is sacrilegious; and the sacrilege is not confined to the subjects of the Archbishop of Westminster, but extends to the whole body diffused throughout the world. And yet our friends form societies to promote their corporate reunion with a Church, which their assertion of the validity of their orders necessarily affirms to be sacrilegious.

A word as to this scheme of 'Corporate Reunion.'
<small>Corporate reunion.</small> It is an impossibility, and the most Utopian of dreams. Union between the Anglican, the Roman, and the Greek Churches, were it possible, would be simply tying together three things—a living body between two corpses. Those things only which are homogeneous can be united, so as to be living parts of one living whole. The subjects of the Greek and

Anglican prelates can only become homogeneous with the subjects of the Catholic Bishops in the various countries throughout the world, by their submission to the Roman Pontiff—the Father of the one family, the Sovereign of the one kingdom, the Head of the one body. Were there to be a corporate submission on the part of the Anglican prelates as representing their Church, that is a scheme of corporate reunion which can be conceived, and a consummation to be devoutly desired. But this can scarcely be their meaning; for to entertain the idea, would be to confess the untenableness of their present position, and to allow the truth of my definition of the Church of England as—a member once existing in the unity of the Mystical Body of Jesus Christ, but now severed from it, soulless, lifeless, dead, and decomposing; or, to vary the similitude,—a branch, once living and fruitful, of the Mystic Vine, but now broken off and lying on the ground, dead and decaying.

But, our friends may say, the severed limb shows signs of life. Yes, signs of life, I admit, but not of organic life—it is of that life which is the result of decomposition, and has centres of its own.

But, at any rate, they may reply, it represents the ancient, the pre-Reformation Church of England, and the 'Anglo-Roman communion,' as they term us, is an exotic and an importation. Again, I admit, it does represent the pre-Reformation Church, but I distinguish: it represents it as a corpse represents him who was once a living being.

I do not defend the position, for I do not think it defensible, inasmuch as I do not believe it to be true, that we represent the pre-Reformation Church of England in the sense of our being a continuation of that body. They represent it, but in the manner I have mentioned.

We are a new mission, straight from Rome — the centre and source and ever-living well-spring of Christianity. Like the mission of St. Augustine, ours is a new wave of Christianity from Rome, to take the place of St. Augustine's, when it was lost in the shifting sands of the Reformation. I think this is made manifest in the fact that we were governed for generations in this country by Vicars Apostolic, until the Hierarchy took their place. The Church of England is the dead branch hewn from the tree, and lying on the ground; we are the new shoot from the parent stem, which has taken its place. In this sense we represent the ancient Church of England; not in an antiquarian sense—to be exhibited on paper, and proved by historical discussion—but in a real and practical sense, inasmuch as that Church and we are one—in origin, in nature, in constitution, in life and thought, and will and action.

In this fact of our being not descended lineally from the pre-Reformation Church, but derived straight from Rome, I see the finger of God, and rejoice day by day with all my heart; for it is a deathblow to the spirit of insularity and nationalism. That spirit was engendered and fostered in past ages by the position of England as an island in the Western Sea, isolated and separated by distance and difficulties of communication from Rome. It broke out at an early period in the Constitutions of Clarendon, it underlay the contentions of the English sovereigns with the Vicar of Christ, and it found its final and legitimate expression in the Statute of Henry VIII.

This is the reason why we love and value everything Roman, simply because it is Roman. It is from no unpatriotic sentiment, and no merely foreign proclivities. Rome is not to us a foreign city. It is our spiritual birthplace and our home. It never can be in reality the capital of Italy: it has a higher destiny. God designed it and made it the capital of Christendom. *Cives Romani sumus*—' We are citizens of Rome.' And what finds its way from Rome hitherward is not an importation, and not an exotic.

Our Anglican friends sometimes object to us that the name of *Roman Catholic* is one which localises us, and signifies that we are something less than Catholic, and not universal or coextensive with the world. They mistake its true meaning. It is not a definition with *Catholic* for its *genus*, and *Roman* for its *differentia*. It resembles what metaphysicians call a transcendental conception; it is *supra omne genus*. It signifies *Roman* in its centre, and *Catholic* in its *circumference*. The centre and the circumference of a sphere are correlatives; they are not the *genus* and *differentia* of its definition.

<small>The name of Roman Catholic.</small>

I accept the term *Roman Catholic* as, in this sense, not a misnomer; but Catholic is our true designation. Others may usurp it, but they cannot make it their own. If they use it, they are misunderstood, and have to condescend to explanation. The Divine Providence has preserved it to us as our own, and we receive it from our enemies as from our brethren. As in the days of St. Augustine, fourteen hundred years ago, so also now. He told the Donatists then, that, ask whom they would to direct them to the nearest Catholic church, and they dared not point the way save to one in communion with Rome. You may here in London, and to-day, apply the same test. Ask your way in the street to the nearest Catholic church, and he whom you ask—be he the highest of High Churchmen—dares not direct you to one of his own magnificent temples, but to a church, however humble and poverty-stricken, which is in communion with Rome. If he directs you otherwise, he knows he has deceived you, and he has the stain of a voluntary deception on his soul.

In this light you see how the terms Anglo-Catholic in England, and Alt-Catholic in Germany, are absurdities and palpable contradictions in terms.

But, to return to the subject of 'Anglican orders.' It is to me, my dear friend, the greatest consolation that they are absolutely invalid; and for this reason —were they valid, England would be probably at this moment under a curse. It would be red with the Blood of our Divine Lord. The guilt of sacrilege would rest upon her, and upon her children. Were they valid, the ministers of the Church of England would be schismatic indeed, but still true priests. In that case, if they said the words of consecration with due intention, they would have the Blessed Sacrament; they would have the Body and Blood of the Divine Victim at their mercy. Now, reflect what— before the recent High-Church movement—was, not the isolated and occasional, but the usual and ordinary practice in disposing of what remained of the bread and wine in the Lord's Supper of the Anglican Church. A record of details I spare you; and it is needless—you know them as well as I do.

The invalidity of Anglican orders a blessing, and a subject of congratulation and thanksgiving.

We, who are certain of the fact that your ministers are laymen, and therefore their 'consecrated elements' but bread and wine, hear of their destination with a smile; did we agree with the High Churchmen, we should think of it with a shudder. But, thanks be to God! England has been saved the guilt and the punishment of such a sin; and the Church of England has never banished the Incarnate Word from her temples, for He has never, since she possessed them, been within their walls.

But, say our Anglican friends, does this wonderful preternatural unity of which you speak, and on which you so much insist, both as a necessary property and as a sufficient note and evidence of the Church of Christ, does it exist? Is it not more apparent than real? Are there not differences among Catholics? And, if they do not appear like ours on the surface, is it not simply because they are kept down and out of sight by an iron authority? What of Dr. Döllinger, Père Hyacinthe, and the Abbé Michaud? _{Recent defections.}

My answer is: They and those who agree with them are no more Catholics than you are. Nay, they are more protestant than you or any hereditary Protestant. Your present position is the result not of your own act, but of the acts of your forefathers; for their position they are individually responsible. They are no more to be objected to us than Henry VIII. or Martin Luther. 'They went out from us, because they were not of us.' The member was mortified before it was amputated. The branch had withered and become barren and lifeless, before it was externally and visibly severed from the Mystic Vine. They had ceased to live with the intellectual and spiritual life of the Body of Christ; and their ultimate separation from its organic system was but the natural issue of this, in the ordinary course of things.

But, you insist, what as to the 'Liberal Catholics'?

Are there not men professedly within the pale of the Catholic and Roman Church, who are nevertheless not at one with her authorities in their belief? It is true. There are such men; and they are in the Church, as St. Augustine says, '*sicut humores in corpore.*'

<small>Liberal Catholics.</small>

Their number is, at the present moment, infinitesimal in proportion to the whole, and it will probably in the future become even less; for as time goes on, they will either assimilate, and be re-absorbed into the intellectual life of the Church, or their divergence will increase, until finally even their organic connection with her will cease.

Their presence within the Church cannot affect her life, for that is guaranteed. It affects her well-being, simply in the same way that a locally diseased part in the human body is apt to communicate the virus to the parts adjacent to, and in contact with it. But living bodies, by a natural force of their life, throw off disease, and cast out from themselves whatever is not homogeneous with their nature, and living with their life.

In any case the presence of such persons within the Church cannot be brought as an argument against the unity of her life and thought and language. Dead branches and withered leaves may long remain outwardly in the unity of living and fruitful vines. Sooner or later they fall to the ground by their own weight, or are pruned away by the knife of the vine-dresser. A similar fate awaits these men.

The Church of God attempts to heal before she puts in the knife. She does not always excise the tumour at its first appearance on the surface; and even when she foresees this necessity in the future, she pauses till she has ascertained how far throughout the body the roots of the tumour extend. This is one reason for her long-suffering patience with Gallicanism. There is a theological distinction between toleration *in ecclesiâ* and toleration *ab ecclesiâ*. That heresy was long tolerated *in* the Church; it was never tolerated *by* the Church. The first was the part of wisdom; the second would have been suicidal. At last its death-warrant was prepared, and its doom was sealed; and now Gallicanism is mouldering in the grave of extinct heresies.

If any one now remains outwardly in communion with the Church, inwardly disbelieving the Vatican doctrine, he is a dishonest person. If he professes his disbelief, he cuts himself off from the Sacraments. If he conceals it, he exists after the manner of a bullet in the human frame; he remains unexpelled, but like a dead thing in a living body, foreign to its nature, apart from its life, receiving nothing from it, and contributing nothing towards its well-being.

Morally, the position of 'Liberal Catholics' is wicked; *intellectually*, it is contemptible. Catholicism is logical, so is Pure Theism; but any position between the two is logically untenable. I can understand a man losing the faith, and falling back upon Pure Theism, and becoming a Deist or Unitarian. He loses his soul, but he preserves his logic. I cannot understand a man relapsing into Protestantism, or into what is equally protestant, 'Liberal Catholicism.' Such a man loses both his soul and his logic.

And yet these are the men who excuse their insubordination on the plea of 'intellectual difficulties.'

This is the bait wherewith they entrap the unwary, and angle for admiration, as well as deprecate censure.

It looks well to have 'intellectual difficulties;' it seems to suppose the possession of intellectual endowments above the average, along with a scrupulous conscience. One's opposition to authority comes before the world as an exigence of one's intellectual superiority.

But, pardon me, difficulties in the way of faith are not intellectual difficulties; they are *moral* difficulties, in those at least who have once possessed the gift of faith. Recollect what I have said about the light of faith; it is a gift of God, and the 'gifts of God are without repentance.' When God gives a grace, He will never take it away, save for moral delinquency. If, then, a man has once had the light of faith, and there is no moral stain or defect in his spiritual life, his spiritual vision will, by a law of its being, grow clearer and clearer, brighter and brighter, until the perfect day. There can be no darkening of an understanding once illuminated by that light, save as a consequence of a moral transgression or shortcoming.

Those 'intellectual difficulties,' then, are wrongly named. They have passed into the intellect, it is true; but they did not begin there, they had their rise in the will. There was an indulgence of the spirit of pride, of insubordination, and impatience of control, before there was difficulty of belief. There was self-will first, and then came private judgment. I forbear to mention those grosser acts of moral depravity which so commonly precede error in matters of faith. We have examples of both spiritual and carnal moral decadence, as the prelude to unbelief, in Henry VIII. and in Martin Luther.

But why, you may fairly ask, do I, in writing to you, a Protestant, expose 'Liberal Catholics'? It is for two reasons. First, because they are Catholics only in name, and Protestants in reality. Their very name of '*Liberal* Catholics' shows them to be something less, and therefore something other than Catholic. Secondly, you may come across them by chance, although, it is true, they are few in number, and they are not quite the men who make converts; and it is well that they should not come before you under false pretences. Do not be deceived by their assumption of intellectual preëminence, their specious professions of historical knowledge and accuracy, and their show of conscientiousness. These are but a cloak for the moral defects of self-confidence, self-will, arrogance, and pride. Far better never be outwardly a member of the Catholic Church than join their ranks, and imbibe their spirit; far better stand before the tribunal of your Maker as a Protestant, than as one of the number of the 'false brethren,' as one who had 'wounded Him in the house of His friends.'

And now I must bring this long Letter to a close. And what are you to do? First, I implore you, place yourself in the presence of your Maker, and realise that you are a *creature*—that all you are and all you have is from Him. This is humility, and if you do not build upon this foundation, you build upon the sand.

Conclusion.

Next, reflect that He is a Spirit, and so are you—that He desires to communicate His Truth to you, and that He has framed your intellect so that it tends to receive it.

Thirdly, remember that His revelation being supernatural, you require supernatural light to apprehend it, and supernatural strength to embrace and retain it. For this you must pray. Without prayer you will do nothing.

Fourthly, that the truths of Pentecost may be proposed to your mind, you need a teacher. 'Faith comet by hearing.' 'The priest's lips shall keep knowledg and thou shalt inquire the law at his mouth.' If this was true of the elder dispensation, how much more true is it not of the Gospel of the God-Man! It is not as a general rule by controversy or study, but by the living action of soul on soul, of a soul full of the light of faith on a soul as yet in the darkness of unbelief, by the hearing of the *truth* from the lips of *authority*, that faith comes.

Fifthly, come then to me, or go to some other priest: it matters not to whom. Our natural abilities and acquirements may vary; but our authority is one, and our teaching is the same. It is not through our powers of persuasion, but by the might of God, that you will see and know.

Sixthly, *act at once*. You are not bound as yet to submit; but you are bound to *inquire*. If you have a shadow of a doubt, the faintest reasonable suspicion that you may be wrong, you are bound, on peril of your soul, not to rest till you are absolutely certain that you are right. 'The night cometh, when no man can work.' To-day may be your last, and—your eternity is at stake.

Seventhly, prepare your soul to meet temptation. You will have suggestions from the great Enemy of Souls, the wisdom of the worldly, and the frailty of fallen nature to contend against.

<small>Temptations to hinder conversion.</small>

Among the wiles of the devil in our day are, 'Go abroad, throw yourself into hard work, and your doubts will disappear.' Yes, I quite grant, your doubts will disappear. But will they be displaced by certainty, and will you have 'the joy and peace of believing'?

Again, 'Take time, and be prudent, whatever you do. Promise me that you will wait for a year, or at least six months, before you take the final step; and that you will not see a Catholic priest, or read a Catholic book, or enter a Catholic church during that time.' Let us look at this. In the first place, are you quite sure that you will be alive six months hence? Already the words may be said of you, 'Thou fool! this night thy soul shall be required of thee.' And then what answer could you give to the question of your Judge, 'Why are you not a Catholic? Why did you stifle instead of solving your doubts? Why did you not at least go on inquiring?'

I agree with the counsel, 'Take time, and be prudent.' You are safe so long as you are earnestly, honestly, and anxiously inquiring; but from the moment that, by God's grace, you see the truth, there is not a moment for delay. Your reason, illuminated by the light of faith, sees, and your judgment declares, that there is on earth a Divine Teacher; your conscience says, 'Submit yourself unreservedly to that teacher;' and every moment thereafter till you resolve, 'I will and do submit myself,' is at the peril of your soul.

You may make promises of delay, and you may confirm them by an oath, if you will. Such promises do not bind you. They are made against the interests of your Maker, and of your own soul. They are null and void, from their nature and in their beginning, rotten in the foundation, and valueless. You were weak to make them, you would be wicked to keep them.

Again, you will have temptations from the possible, nay, almost inevitable consequences of your conversion, in the rude wrench given to the friendships of years and to family ties, and which may issue in their disruption; in the damage done to your temporal position and prospects, involving those also who depend on and are very near and dear to you. To have to leave all, in order to follow the Divine Teacher, has been the lot of many, who, in late years, have received the grace of Divine faith.

Whether you will have to face this or not, at any rate you must have the will to bear the cross, if it be laid upon you. But fear not! He, who has Himself borne the Cross, never lays a cross upon any of His children without first calculating both its weight and their weakness, and bestowing an adequate grace.

Those disturbances in families, which are so often the result of the conversion of one of the members to the Catholic Church, are regarded by those without as an argument against that Church; to us they are an additional argument for its oneness with Him who said: 'I came not to send peace on the earth, but the sword; for I came to set a man at variance against his father, and the daughter against her mother, and the daughter-in-law against her mother-in-law; and a man's enemies shall be they of his own household. He that loveth father or mother more than Me, is not worthy of Me; and he that loveth son or daughter more than Me, is not worthy of Me; and he that taketh not up his cross and followeth Me, is not worthy of Me. He that receiveth you, receiveth me; and he that receiveth Me, receiveth Him that sent Me.'

So also we are said to be inimical to governments. Men said the same of Him — that this man was not Cæsar's friend.

Both accusations are false. The Catholic Church recognises and supports authority, wherever found, in every form, civil and social: 'for there is no power but from God, and those that are, are ordained of God; therefore he that resisteth the power, resisteth the ordinance of God; and they that resist, purchase to themselves damnation.' The Church enforces the legitimate authority alike of the sovereign, of the husband, and of the father; but she at the same time proclaims and protects the personal rights of the subject, of the wife, and of the child. And, above all, she is careful as to the rights of God, and when those are interfered with by any pretensions of authority, either civil or social, she disregards such pretensions in the interests of Him who is supreme, and Lord over all.

Now God has a right to the submission of every one of His intelligent creatures; and every one of these has an individual responsibility in regard to such submission. When, therefore, any human being receives the light of Divine faith, and recognises the one Divine Teacher, he is bound to submission, on peril of his soul, whatever civil ruler, husband, or father may say to the contrary. The relationship between husband and wife, and between parent and child, is very close; but the relationship between Creator and creature is closer still. We must render to Cæsar the things which are Cæsar's; but we must first render to God the things which are God's.

It is our clear perception of the absolute supremacy of God over the human soul, which accounts for our practice in dealing with individual converts, a practice which draws down upon us so much animadversion and obloquy; and it is a practical forgetfulness of this primary principle which lies at the root of the world's misapprehension and condemnation of our conduct, as an invasion of its civil and social rights.

The world requires the consent of relations as a

condition of submission to the Catholic Church; and thinks it an outrage on the rights of society and of the family that such consent should not be first asked and obtained.

But if we look at the matter calmly, can human relations, however close, *give consent?* How can they give that which they cannot withhold? The very notion supposes the equality, nay, the superiority of their claims to those of God. It is a practical denial of His supremacy.

I admit that there are cases when it is well to inform relations of the contemplated submission; but this, as a measure of policy and prudence; as a question of right, I deny the obligation.

Farther, if the individual believes or suspects that there will be opposition on the part of his relations, and he is conscious of his own frailty—and self-distrust belongs to humility—what right has he to imperil his soul by placing himself in what may be to him, through his weakness, a proximate occasion of mortal sin?

His submission is a matter of individual responsibility. He will stand alone before God, to be judged concerning it; and while we say '*Our* Father,' we say also, 'I believe.'

I have spoken of this matter at some length, because it is one of the common objections brought against our converts, and the method and circumstances of their conversion; and one which Protestants, universally, fail to understand.

Another, is the suddenness, the 'indecent haste,' it is sometimes called, of their submission, at the last. But surely, it must be at a particular moment of time when the truth first breaks upon the mind in all its convincing clearness, and when the obligation of submission first presses upon the conscience with all its constraining force; and when that moment arrives, what reason remains, and what excuse for delay?

You see, then, my friend, your position at this moment. You are a branch severed from the Mystic Vine; a member apart from the Mystical Body. You must be engrafted into the One Vine, and joined to the One Body, that you may have life in you.

A cunning workman may take a piece of wood, and carve it into the likeness of a tree, and that so skilfully as to deceive the eyes of his fellow-men, and he may plant it in the ground, but it will not take root downward, and bear fruit upward. He may take a piece of wax, and mould it into the likeness of a man, and again he may deceive the eyes of his fellow-men, but he cannot make it breathe, and think, and will, and act. Those are vital acts, indicative of, and the result of life; and He alone can bestow life who is the Lord of life, and in whose Hands are the issues of life and death. Impossibility of reformation by men of a divine creation.

How, then, can men reform that which they are impotent to create — a living thing?

They may destroy, but they cannot reform a divine work. A man may cut into chips a living tree; but he is powerless to reform a living tree out of the lifeless chips. He may take to pieces a living body, but he cannot put it together again, and restore the life which has vanished by his act. And until men can accomplish this in the natural order, with the forms of sensitive or vegetative life, we may well pause till we believe it possible that they can, by act of parliament, take to pieces, reform, and reconstruct any part of the living Church of the living God. The only reformation possible is that which comes from within, and is the result of that intrinsic and natural power which belongs to her, in common with every living thing, of casting out foreign elements, and throwing off disease.

She is visible, before your eyes, in her living oneness, she is her own evidence; and never has that evidence been more thrust home on the intelligence of the world than in our day. The fact of living alongside of the Vatican Council was an 'external grace,' such as is vouchsafed to the human race only at intervals during the centuries. Three hundred years had passed since the collective Episcopate of the world met in council; and the faith which it professed at Trent it professed with unhesitating, undoubting unanimity at Rome. What grander, what more striking moral spectacle of living unity could be seen or imagined than the recitation by the Bishops of the Creed of Pope Pius the Fourth?

To be contemporary with the Vatican Council a great 'external grace.'

If there could be a grander, it was this—the adhesion and submission of the Prelates who, in the exercise of their wisdom and prudence, in the excess of their anxiety and jealous care for the spiritual welfare of their individual flocks, doubted, even up to the morning of the 18th of July, as to the opportuneness of the definition, that is to say, of the advisability of defining the dogma at the present time, having regard to all the circumstances of the day.

Their attitude and conduct is inexplicable to the world without. The world exerted itself to the utmost, used all its arts in cabinets and in cafés, in salons and in newspapers, intriguing and threatening, plotting and prophesying. Rumours of difference of opinion within the Council floated outwards on the air; and the world, in its wisdom, argued difference of faith. It congratulated itself that it had a party even in the bosom of its antagonist; and the world loved those whom it fondly supposed to be its own. It was loud in its expressions of admiration and praise of the men of ability and learning, of prudence and sagacity, of conscientiousness and fidelity to truth, who were to fight its battle against the hot-headed, imperious, ignorant, but crafty champions of authority.

The world has discovered its mistake; and its admiration and praise is turned into contempt and blame.

Instead of resulting in the schism which it anticipated, the difference of *opinion* within the Council has but made more striking the unanimity of the teachers of the nations in the faith of Pentecost. It was a background of shadows painted in by the Hand of God, to throw out into clearer relief the oneness of His Church.

What that Church teaches, I need not enter on now. It would be premature, and it would be useless. It would be beginning at the wrong end, and a waste of your time and mine. Were I to endeavour to persuade you of the truth of the teacher, by proving to you the truth of the teaching, the issue would be valueless, and my labour in vain.

This is the method of our imitators. They adopt our *doctrines*, one by one; and then suppose that they *believe* our *doctrine*. That doctrine is, like the moral law, indivisible. 'Whosoever shall keep the whole law, but offend in one point, is become guilty of all.' So also whosoever should hold all our doctrines, save one, believes not at all. He possesses a bundle of opinions, having each a Roman flavour; but he does not possess the one faith of Rome. Were such an one to find his way into the Church, his would not be a conversion: for it would be, not by way of *submission*, but by way of *agreement*. There would be two high contracting parties; he on the one side, and the Church of God on the other. And what would be the issue? The Church might one day define some truth which he had not contemplated; and he would refuse to accept her definition, as not included within the terms of the concordat. He would, all his life long, have 'difficulties,' and talk about being 'obliged to believe;' and ultimately he would depart by the door through which he entered. He would 'go out from us,' for the simple reason that he was never 'of us.'

No; I shall teach you carefully the whole cycle of Christian doctrine; but not until you have recognised the Divine Teacher, and submitted yourself unreservedly to her Divine authority. To tell you her doctrines now would be merely to gratify your curiosity; or, at most, to give you *information*. It would not be *teaching;* for that supposes a disciple submissive to his teacher.

You will have to be prepared for the Sacraments, one by one, as you approach them.

For your reception a knowledge of two suffices, of Baptism and Penance; and that is required, because those two form part of the order of your reception.

You will have, it is true, to profess your faith in the various articles of the Christian doctrine, as laid down in the Creed of Pope Pius; but then, not because you have examined them, and they severally commend themselves to you, but because they are proposed to you by the Divine Teacher. This is the one intelligent ground of your belief. If you believe in her Divine authority, you thereby implicitly believe in the infallibility of her doctrine.

May God grant you the twofold grace, of light to

see His truth, and of strength to embrace it, whatever it may cost you!

Believe me always

Most truly yours,

WILLIAM HUMPHREY

SELECTION

FROM

BURNS & OATES'

Catalogue

OF

PUBLICATIONS.

LONDON: BURNS AND OATES, Ld.

28 Orchard St., W.

1895.

Latest Publications.

A Retreat: Consisting of Thirty-three Discourses with Meditations, intended for the use of the Clergy, Religious, and others. By the RIGHT REV. JOHN CUTHBERT HEDLEY, O.S.B., Bishop of Newport and Menevia. Second edition. In handsome half-leather binding. Crown 8vo, price 6s.

Journals kept during Times of Retreat. By Father John Morris, S.J. Selected and edited by Father J. H. Pollen, S.J. New volume, Quarterly Series. Cloth 6s.

The Sacred Heart, and other Sermons. By the REV. ALFRED FAWKES. Red buckram, gilt, 2s. 6d.

Bernadette of Lourdes. A Mystery. Translated from the French of E. POUVILLON by HENRY O'SHEA. Blue buckram, gilt, 2/6.

The Inner Life of Father Thomas Burke, O.P. By a Dominican Friar of the English Province. Dark green buckram, gilt, 2s.

The Life of St. Philip Neri. Translated from the Italian of CARDINAL CAPECELATRO. By the REV. THOMAS ALDER POPE, of the Oratory. Second Edition. In two Vols., Price 12s. 6d.

Purgatory. Illustrated by the Lives and Legends of the Saints. From the French of Father F. X. Schouppe, S.J. Cloth, 6s.

"We feel absolutely confident that Father Schouppe's work will soon become one of our most popular works on Purgatory, and that we shall ere long have to notice its second edition."—*Tablet.*

The Jewish Race in Ancient and Roman History. Translated from the 11th corrected edition of A. RENDU, LL.D., by THERESA CROOK. Crown 8vo, cloth, 6s.

Literary and Biographical History; or, Bibliographical Dictionary of the English Catholics. From the Breach with Rome, in 1534, to the present time. By JOSEPH GILLOW. Vol. IV., Cloth, demy 8vo, 15s. Now ready Vols. I., II., and III., in uniform style, 15s. each.

(The fifth and concluding volume will follow shortly.)

History of the Church of England. From the Accession of Henry VIII. to the Death of Queen Elizabeth. By MARY H. Allies. Crown 8vo, cloth, 3s. 6d. Being a Sequel to the History of the Church in England from the Beginning of the Christian Era to the Accession of Henry VIII. By the same Author. Crown 8vo, cloth, 6s.

No. 1.   1895.

SELECTION
FROM
BURNS AND OATES' CATALOGUE OF PUBLICATIONS.

ALLIES, T. W. (K.C.S.G.)

	£ s. d.
A Life's Decision. Crown 8vo, cloth	0 5 0
The Formation of Christendom.	
Vol. I.—Popular Edition. Crown 8vo, cloth.	0 5 0
Vols. II. and III. Demy 8vo, . . . each	0 10 0
Church and State as seen in the Formation of Christendom, 8vo, pp. 472, cloth . (out of print.)	
The Throne of the Fisherman, built by the Carpenter's Son, the Root, the Bond, and the Crown of Christendom. Demy 8vo	0 10 6
The Holy See and the Wandering of the Nations. Demy 8vo	0 10 6
Peter's Rock in Mohammed's Flood. Demy 8vo	0 10 6

"It would be quite superfluous at this hour of the day to recommend Mr. Allies' writings to English Catholics. Those of our readers who remember the article on his writings in the *Katholik*, know that he is esteemed in Germany as one of our foremost writers."—*Dublin Review.*

ALLIES, MARY.

	£ s. d.
Leaves from St. John Chrysostom. With introduction by T. W. Allies, K.C.S.G. Crown 8vo, cloth.	0 6 0

"Miss Allies' 'Leaves' are delightful reading; the English is remarkably pure and graceful; page after page reads as if it were original. No commentator, Catholic or Protestant, has ever surpassed St. John Chrysostom in the knowledge of Holy Scripture, and his learning was of a kind which is of service now as it was at the time when the inhabitants of a great city hung on his words."—*Tablet.*

	£ s. d.
History of the Church in England, from the beginning of the Christian Era to the accession of Henry VIII. Crown 8vo, cloth	0 6 0
The Second Part, to the End of Queen Elizabeth's Reign. Crown 8vo, cloth	0 3 6

"Miss Allies has in this volume admirably compressed the substance, or such as was necessary to her purpose, of a number of authorities, judiciously selected. . . . As a narrative the volume is capitally a written, as a summary it is skilful, and not its least excellence is its value as an index of the best available sources which deal with the period it covers."—*Birmingham Daily Gazette.*

ANNUS SANCTUS:

	£ s. d.
Hymns of the Church for the Ecclesiastical Year. Translated from the Sacred Offices by various Authors, with Modern, Original, and other Hymns, and an Appendix of Earlier Versions. Selected and Arranged by ORBY SHIPLEY, M.A. Plain cloth, lettered	0 5 6

ANSWERS TO ATHEISTS: OR NOTES ON
Ingersoll. By the Rev. A. Lambert, (over 100,000 copies
sold in America). Twelfth edition. Paper. . . £0 0 6
Cloth 0 1 0

BAKER, VEN. FATHER AUGUSTIN.
Holy Wisdom; or, Directions for the Prayer of Contemplation, &c. Extracted from Treatises written by the Ven. Father F. Augustin Baker, O.S.B., and edited by Abbot Sweeney, D.D. Beautifully bound in half leather 0 6 0

"We earnestly recommend this most beautiful work to all our readers. We are sure that every community will use it as a constant manual. If any persons have friends in convents, we cannot conceive a better present they can make them, or a better claim they can have on their prayers, than by providing them with a copy."—*Weekly Register.*

BOWDEN, REV. H. S. (of the Oratory) Edited by.
Dante's Divina Commedia: Its scope and value. From the German of FRANCIS HETTINGER, D.D. With an engraving of Dante. 2nd Edition. . . 0 10 6

"All that Venturi attempted to do has been now approached with far greater power and learning by Dr. Hettinger, who, as the author of the 'Apologie des Christenthums,' and as a great Catholic theologian, is eminently well qualified for the task he has undertaken."—*The Saturday Review.*

Natural Religion. Being Vol. I. of Dr. Hettinger's Evidences of Christianity. With an Introduction on Certainty. Second edition. Crown 8vo, cloth 0 7 6

"As an able statement of the Catholic Doctrine of Certitude, and a defence, from the Romanist point of view, of the truth of Christianity, it was well worth while translating Dr. Franz Hettinger's 'Apologie des Christenthums,' of which the first part is now published."—*Scotsman.*

Revealed Religion. Being the Second Volume of the above work. With an Introduction on the "Assent of Faith." Crown 8vo, cloth, ... 0 7 6

BRIDGETT, REV. T. E. (C.SS.R.).
Discipline of Drink 0 3 6

"The historical information with which the book abounds gives evidence of deep research and patient study, and imparts a permanent interest to the volume, which will elevate it to a position of authority and importance enjoyed by few of its compeers."—*The Arrow.*

Our Lady's Dowry; how England Won that Title. New and Enlarged Edition. 0 5 0

"This book is the ablest vindication of Catholic devotion to Our Lady, drawn from tradition, that we know of in the English language."—*Tablet.*

Ritual of the New Testament. An essay on the principles and origin of Catholic Ritual in reference to the New Testament. Third edition . . . 0 5 0

The Life of the Blessed John Fisher. With a reproduction of the famous portrait of Blessed JOHN FISHER by HOLBEIN, and other Illustrations, 2nd Ed. 0 7 6

"The Life of Blessed John Fisher could hardly fail to be interesting and instructive. Sketched by Father Bridgett's practised pen the portrait of this holy martyr is no less vividly displayed in the printed pages of the book than in the wonderful picture of Holbein, which forms the frontispiece."—*Tablet.*

BRIDGETT REV. T. E. (C.SS.R.)—*continued*.

The True Story of the Catholic Hierarchy deposed by Queen Elizabeth, with fuller Memoirs of its Last Two Survivors. By the Rev. T. E. BRIDGETT, C.SS.R., and the late Rev. T. F. KNOX, D.D., of the London Oratory. Crown 8vo, cloth, £0 7 6

"We gladly acknowledge the value of this work on a subject which has been obscured by prejudice and carelessness."—*Saturday Review.*

The Life and Writings of Blessed Thomas More, Lord Chancellor of England and Martyr under Henry VIII. With Portrait of the Martyr taken from the Crayon Sketch made by Holbein in 1527. 2nd Ed. 0 7 6

"Father Bridgett has followed up his valuable Life of Bishop Fisher with a still more valuable Life of Thomas More. It is, as the title declares, a study not only of the life, but also of the writings of Sir Thomas. Father Bridgett has considered him from every point of view, and the result is, it seems to us, a more complete and finished portrait of the man, mentally and physically, than has been hitherto presented."—*Athenæum.*

The Wisdom and Wit of Blessed Thomas More . . 0 6 0

"It would be hard to find another such collection of true wisdom and keen, pungent, yet gentle wit and humour, as this volume contains."—*American Catholic Quarterly.*

BRIDGETT, REV. T. E. (C.SS.R.), Edited by.

Souls Departed. By CARDINAL ALLEN. First published in 1565, now edited in modern spelling by the Rev. T. E. Bridgett 0 6 0

BROWNLOW, BISHOP

A Memoir of the late Sir James Marshall, C.M.G., K.C.S.G., taken chiefly from his own letters. With Portrait. Crown 8vo, cloth . . 0 3 6
Lectures on Slavery and Serfdom in Europe. Cloth 0 3 6

"The general impression left by the perusal of this interesting book is one of great fairness and thorough grasp of the subject."—*Month*

BUCKLER, REV. REGINALD, (O.P.)

The Perfection of Man by Charity. A Spiritual Treatise. Second edition. Crown 8vo. cloth 0 5 0

"The object of Father Buckler's useful and interesting book is to lay down the principles of the spiritual life for the benefit of Religious and Seculars. The book is written in an easy and effective style, and the apt citations with which he enriches his pages would of themselves make the treatise valuable."—*Dublin Review.*

CARMINA MARIANA.

An English Anthology in Verse in honour of the Blessed Virgin Mary. Edited by ORBY SHIPLEY, M.A. Second and cheaper Edition. Crown 8vo, 472 pp., bound in blue and red cloth . . . 0 7 6

"Contains everything at all worthy of the theme that has been written in English verse to the praise of the Blessed Virgin Mary from Chaucer's time to the present year, including the best translations from Latin, French and other languages."—*Irish Monthly.*

CATHOLIC BELIEF: OR, A SHORT AND
Simple Exposition of Catholic Doctrine. By the
Very Rev. Joseph Faà di Bruno, D.D. Twelfth
edition . . . . . Price 6d.; post free, £0 0 8½
Cloth, lettered, ... 0 0 10

CHALLONER, BISHOP.
Meditations for every day in the year. Revised and
edited by the Right Rev. John Virtue, D.D., Bishop
of Portsmouth. 7th edition. 8vo . . . 0 3 0
And in other bindings.

COLERIDGE, REV. H. J. (S.J.) *(See Quarterly Series.)*

DALE, REV. J. D. HILARIUS.
Ceremonial according to the Roman Rite. Translated
from the Italian of JOSEPH BALDESCHI, Master of
Ceremonies of the Basilica of St. Peter at Rome;
with the Pontifical Offices of a Bishop in his own
diocese, compiled from the "Cæremoniale Episcoporum"; to which are added various other Func-
tions and copious explanatory Notes; the whole
harmonized with the latest Decrees of the Sacred Con-
gregation of Rites. New and revised edition. Cloth, 0 6 6

The Sacristan's Manual; or, Handbook of Church
Furniture, Ornament, &c. Harmonized with the
most approved commentaries on the Roman Ceremonial and latest Decrees of the Sacred Congrega-
tion of Rites. Cloth 0 2 6

DEVAS, C. S.
Studies of Family Life: a contribution to Social
Science. Crown 8vo 0 5 0

"We recommend these pages and the remarkable evidence brought
together in them to the careful attention of all who are interested in
the well-being of our common humanity."—*Guardian.*
"Both thoughtful and stimulating."—*Saturday Review.*

DRANE, AUGUSTA THEODOSIA, Edited by.
The Autobiography of Archbishop Ullathorne. Demy
8vo, cloth. Second edition 0 7 6

"As a plucky Yorkshireman, as a sailor, as a missionary, as a
great traveller, as a ravenous reader, and as a great prelate, Dr.
Ullathorne was able to write down most fascinating accounts of his
experiences. The book is full of shrewd glimpses from a Roman point
of view of the man himself, of the position of Roman Catholics in this
country, of the condition of the country, of the Colonies, and of the
Anglican Church in various parts of the world, in the earlier half of
this century."—*Guardian.*

The Letters of Archbishop Ullathorne. (Sequel
to the *Autobiography.*) 2nd Edit. Demy 8vo, cloth 0 9 0
"Compiled with admirable judgment for the purpose of displaying
in a thousand various ways the real man who was Archbishop
Ullathorne."—*Tablet.*

EYRE MOST REV. CHARLES, (Abp. of Glasgow).
The History of St. Cuthbert : or, An Account of his Life, Decease, and Miracles. Third edition. Illustrated with maps, charts, &c., and handsomely bound in cloth. Royal 8vo £0 14 0

"A handsome, well appointed volume, in every way worthy of its illustrious subject. . . . The chief impression of the whole is the picture of a great and good man drawn by a sympathetic hand."—*Spectator.*

FABER, REV. FREDERICK WILLIAM, (D.D.)
All for Jesus	0	5	0
Bethlehem	0	7	0
Blessed Sacrament	0	7	6
Creator and Creature	0	6	0
Ethel's Book of the Angels.	0	5	0
Foot of the Cross	0	6	0
Growth in Holiness	0	6	0
Hymns	0	6	0
Notes on Doctrinal and Spiritual Subjects, 2 vols.	0	10	0
Poems	0	5	0
Precious Blood	0	5	0
Sir Lancelot	0	5	0
Spiritual Conferences	0	6	0
Life and Letters of Frederick William Faber, D.D., Priest of the Oratory of St. Philip Neri. By John Edward Bowden of the same Congregation . .	0	6	0

FAWKES, REV. ALFRED.
The Sacred Heart, and other Sermons. Red buckram, gilt 0 2 6

"Nor do we wonder at the fascination which Father Fawkes's sermons must have for a man of letters, if they at all approached in power and charm those which are brought together in the little first volume he has put to press. Every page of these sermons shows him to be an original and cultivated Catholic thinker. The substance of his discourses never wanders astray from the unchanging doctrines of the Church, and yet there is found throughout them all a freshness of view as welcome as it is uncommon. This preacher has something to say—something worth saying that he wants to say."—*Weekly Register.*

FOLEY, REV. HENRY, (S.J.)
Records of the English Province of the Society of Jesus. Vol. I., Series I. . . . . . net	1	6	0
Vol. II., Series II., III., IV. . . . net	1	6	0
Vol. III., Series V., VI., VII., VIII. . . net	1	10	0
Vol. IV. Series IX., X., XI. . . . net	1	6	0
Vol. V., Series XII. with nine Photographs of Martyrs . . . . net	1	10	0
Vol. VI., Diary and Pilgrim-Book of the English College, Rome . . . . net	1	6	0
Vol. VII. Part the First : General Statistics of the Province; with Biographical Notices and 20 Photographs . . . . net	1	6	0
Vol. VII. Part the Second : Collectanea, Completed ; With Appendices. Catalogues of Assumed and Real Names: Annual Letters; Biographies and Miscellanea. . . . . net	1	6	0

"As a biographical dictionary of English Jesuits, it deserves a place in every well-selected library, and, as a collection of marvellous occurrences, persecutions, martyrdoms, and evidences of the results of faith, amongst the books of all who belong to the Catholic Church."—*Genealogist.*

FORMBY, REV. HENRY.
Monotheism: in the main derived from the Hebrew nation and the Law of Moses. The Primitive Religion of the City of Rome. An historical Investigation. Demy 8vo £0 5 0

FRANCIS DE SALES, ST.: THE WORKS OF.
Translated into the English Language by the Very Rev. Canon Mackey, O.S.B., under the direction of the Right Rev. Bishop Hedley, O.S.B.
Vol. I. Letters to Persons in the World. 3rd Ed. . 0 6 0
"The letters must be read in order to comprehend the charm and sweetness of their style."—*Tablet.*
Vol. II.—The Treatise on the Love of God. Father Carr's translation of 1630 has been taken as a basis, but it has been modernized and thoroughly revised and corrected. 2nd Edition 0 6 0
"To those who are seeking perfection by the path of contemplation this volume will be an armoury of help."—*Saturday Review.*
Vol. III. The Catholic Controversy. . . . 0 6 0
"No one who has not read it can conceive how clear, how convincing, and how well adapted to our present needs are these controversial leaves.'"—*Tablet.*
Vol. IV. Letters to Persons in Religion, with introduction by Bishop Hedley on "St. Francis de Sales and the Religious State." 2nd Edition . . . 0 6 0
"The sincere piety and goodness, the grave wisdom, the knowledge of human nature, the tenderness for its weakness, and the desire for its perfection that pervade the letters, make them pregnant of instruction for all serious persons. The translation and editing have been admirably done."—*Scotsman.*

GALLWEY, REV. PETER, (S.J.)
Precious Pearl of Hope in the Mercy of God, The. Translated from the Italian. With Preface by the Rev. Father Gallwey. Cloth 0 4 6
Lectures on Ritualism and on the Anglican Orders. 2 vols. (Or may be had separately.) 0 8 0
Salvage from the Wreck. A few Memories of the Dead, preserved in Funeral Discourses. With Portraits. Crown 8vo 0 7 6

GIBSON, REV. H.
Catechism Made Easy. Being an Explanation of the Christian Doctrine. 9th Edition. 2 vols., cloth. . 0 7 6
"This work must be of priceless worth to any who are engaged in any form of catechetical instruction. It is the best book of the kind that we have seen in English."—*Irish Monthly.*

GILLOW, JOSEPH.
Literary and Biographical History, or, Bibliographical Dictionary of the English Catholics. From the Breach with Rome, in 1534, to the Present Time. Vols. I., II. III. and IV. cloth, demy 8vo . . each 0 15 0
5th, and concluding vol. in preparation.
"The patient research of Mr. Gillow, his conscientious record of minute particulars, and especially his exhaustive bibliographical information in connection with each name, are beyond praise."—*British Quarterly Review.*
The Haydock Papers. Illustrated. Demy 8vo . 0 7 6
"We commend this collection to the attention of every one that is interested in the records of the sufferings and struggles of our ancestors to hand down the faith to their children."—*Tablet*
St. Thomas' Priory; or, the Story of St. Austin's, Stafford. With Three Illustrations. Tastefully bound in half leather 0 5 0

GLANCEY, REV. M. F.

Characteristics from the Writings of Archbishop Ullathorne, together with a Bibliographical Account of the Archbishop's Works. Crown 8vo, cloth . . £0 6 0

"The Archbishop's thoughts are expressed in choice, rich language, which, pleasant as it is to read, must have been additionally so to hear. We have perused this book with interest, and have no hesitation in recommending our readers to possess themselves of it."—*Birmingham Weekly Mercury.*

GRADWELL, MONSIGNOR.

Succat, The Story of Sixty Years of the Life of St. Patrick. Crown 8vo, cloth 0 5 0

"A work at once bright, picturesque, and truthful."—*Tablet.*
"We most heartily commend this book to all lovers of St. Patrick."—*Irish Ecclesiastical Record.*

GROWTH IN THE KNOWLEDGE OF OUR LORD.

Meditations for every Day in the Year, exclusive of those for Festivals, Days of Retreat, &c. Adapted from the original of Abbé de Brandt, by Sister Mary Fidelis. A new and Improved Edition, in 3 Vols. Sold only in sets. Price per set, ... 1 2 6

"The praise, though high, bestowed on these excellent meditations by the Bishop of Salford is well deserved. The language, like good spectacles, spreads treasures before our vision without attracting attention to itself."—*Dublin Review.*

HEDLEY, BISHOP.

Our Divine Saviour, and other Discourses. Crown 8vo 0 6 0

"A distinct and noteworthy feature of these sermons is, we certainly think, their freshness—freshness of thought, treatment, and style; nowhere do we meet pulpit commonplace or hackneyed phrase—everywhere, on the contrary, it is the heart of the preacher pouring out to his flock his own deep convictions, enforcing them from the 'Treasures, old and new,' of a cultivated mind."—*Dublin Review.*

A Retreat: consisting of Thirty-three Discourses with Meditations, intended for the use of the Clergy, Religious, and others. Crown 8vo, half leather . 0 6 0

"This 'Retreat,' which will remain as a treasure with Catholics of English speech, shows forth once more, and very attractively, his (Dr. Hedley's) qualifications as a preacher and a guide of souls. It gives amplest evidence of his piety and his literary gift, his keen insight into the motives and the weaknesses of the human heart, and withal such a winning humility as leaves the erring one unwounded, though he is enlightened and rebuked."—*Weekly Register.*

INNER LIFE OF FATHER THOMAS BURKE, O.P.

By a Dominican Friar of the English Province. Dark green buckram, gilt. 0 2 0

"In this little work the writer has endeavoured to depict that side of Father Burke's character which, if it is least known, gives the truer as well as the higher idea of the well-known preacher of fifteen years ago.
"It is a singularly pleasing picture of a most attractive character, in which humour, humility, and piety each found an appropriate place."—*Scotsman.*

KING, FRANCIS.

The Church of my Baptism, and why I returned to it. Crown 8vo, cloth 0 2 6

"Altogether a book of an excellent spirit, written with freshness and distinction."—*Weekly Register.*

LEE, REV. F. G., D.D. (of All Saints, Lambeth.)
Edward the Sixth: Supreme Head. Second edition.
Crown 8vo . . . . . . , . . £0 6 0
"In vivid interest and in literary power, no less than in solid historical value, Dr. Lee's present work comes fully up to the standard of its predecessors; and to say that is to bestow high praise. The book evinces Dr. Lee's customary diligence of research in amassing facts, and his rare artistic power in welding them into a harmonious and effective whole."—*John Bull.*

LIGUORI, ST. ALPHONSUS.
New and Improved Translation of the Complete Works of St. Alphonsus, edited by the late Bishop Coffin:--
Vol. I. The Christian Virtues, and the Means for Obtaining them. Cloth 0 3 0
Or separately:—
  1. The Love of our Lord Jesus Christ . . . 0 1 0
  2. Treatise on Prayer. *(In the ordinary editions a great part of this work is omitted)* . . . 0 1 0
  3. A Christian's rule of Life 0 1 0
Vol. II. The Mysteries of the Faith—The Incarnation; containing Meditations and Devotions on the Birth and Infancy of Jesus Christ, &c., suited for Advent and Christmas. 0 2 6
Vol. III. The Mysteries of the Faith—The Blessed Sacrament 0 2 6
Vol. IV. Eternal Truths—Preparation for Death . 0 2 6
Vol. V. The Redemption—Meditations on the Passion. 0 2 6
Vol. VI. Glories of Mary. New edition . . . 0 3 6
Reflections on Spiritual Subjects . . . 0 2 6

LIVIUS, REV. T. (M.A., C.SS.R.)
St. Peter, Bishop of Rome; or, the Roman Episcopate of the Prince of the Apostles, proved from the Fathers, History and Chronology, and illustrated by arguments from other sources. Dedicated to his Eminence Cardinal Newman. Demy 8vo, cloth . 0 12 0
"A book which deserves careful attention. In respect of literary qualities, such as effective arrangement, and correct and lucid diction, this essay, by an English Catholic scholar, is not unworthy of Cardinal Newman, to whom it is dedicated."—*The Sun.*
Explanation of the Psalms and Canticles in the Divine Office. By ST. ALPHONSUS LIGUORI. Translated from the Italian by THOMAS LIVIUS, C.SS.R. With a Preface by his Eminence Cardinal MANNING. Crown 8vo, cloth 0 7 6
" To nuns and others who know little or no Latin, the book will be of immense importance."—*Dublin Review.*
"Father Livius has in our opinion even improved on the original, so far as the arrangement of the book goes. New priests will find it especially useful."—*Month.*
Mary in the Epistles; or, The Implicit Teaching of the Apostles concerning the Blessed Virgin, set forth in devout comments on their writings. Illustrated from Fathers and other Authors, and prefaced by introductory Chapters. Crown 8vo, cloth 0 5 0
The Blessed Virgin in the Fathers of the First Six Centuries. With a Preface by CARD. VAUGHAN. Cloth 0 12 0

"Father Livius could hardly have laid at the feet of Our Blessed Patroness a more fitting tribute than to have placed side by side with the work of his fellow-Redemptorist on the 'Dowry of Mary,' this volume, in which we hear the combined voices of the Fathers of the first six centuries united in speaking the praise of the Mother of God."—*Dublin Review*.

MANNING, CARDINAL. Popular Edition of the Works of

	£	s.	d.
Four Great Evils of the Day. 6th edition	0	2	6
Fourfold Sovereignty of God. 4th edition	0	2	6
Glories of the Sacred Heart. 6th edition	0	4	0
Grounds of Faith. 10th edition	0	1	6
Independence of the Holy See. 2nd edition	0	2	6
Internal Mission of the Holy Ghost. 5th edition	0	5	0
Miscellanies. 3 vols. the set	0	18	0
Pastime Papers. 2nd edition	0	2	6
Religio Viatoris. 4th edition	0	1	6
Sermons on Ecclesiastical Subjects. Vol. I.	0	6	0
(Vols. II. and III. out of Print.)			
Sin and its Consequences. 8th edition	0	4	0
Temporal Mission of the Holy Ghost. 3rd edition	0	5	0
True Story of the Vatican Council. 2nd edition	0	2	6
The Eternal Priesthood. 11th edition	0	2	6
The Office of the Church in the Higher Catholic Education. A Pastoral Letter	0	0	6
Workings of the Holy Spirit in the Church of England. Reprint of a letter addressed to Dr. Pusey in 1864	0	1	6
Lost Sheep Found. A Sermon	0	0	6
Rights and Dignity of Labour	0	0	1

The Westminster Series

In handy pocket size. All bound in cloth.

The Blessed Sacrament, the Centre of Immutable Truth	0	1	0
Confidence in God.	0	1	0
Holy Gospel of Our Lord Jesus Christ according to St. John.	0	1	0
Love of Jesus to Penitents.	0	1	0
Office of the Holy Ghost under the Gospel	0	1	0
Holy Ghost the Sanctifier	0	2	0

MANNING, CARDINAL, Edited by.

Life of the Curé of Ars. Popular edition	0	2	6

MEDAILLE, REV. P.

Meditations on the Gospels or Every Day in the Year. Translated into English from the new Edition, enlarged by the Besançon Missionaries, under the direction of the Rev. W. H. Eyre, S.J. Cloth . . . 0 6 0

(This work has already been translated into Latin, Italian, Spanish, German, and Dutch.)

"We have carefully examined these Meditations, and are fain to confess that we admire them very much. They are short, succinct, pithy, always to the point, and wonderfully suggestive."—*Tablet*.

MEYNELL, ALICE.

Lourdes: Yesterday, to-day, and to-morrow. Translated from the French of Daniel Barbé by Alice Meynell. With twelve full pages water colour drawings by Hoffbauer, reproduced in colours. Royal 8vo, blue buckram, gilt 0 6 0

MORRIS, REV. JOHN (S.J., F.S.A.)

Letter Books of Sir Amias Poulet, keeper of Mary
Queen of Scots. Demy 8vo . . . . net £0 3 6
Two Missionaries under Elizabeth 0 14 0
The Catholics under Elizabeth 0 14 0
The Life of Father John Gerard, S.J. Third edition,
rewritten and enlarged 0 14 0
The Life and Martyrdom of St. Thomas Becket. Second
and enlarged edition. In one volume, large post 8vo,
cloth, pp. xxxvi., 632, ... 0 12 6
or bound in two parts, cloth 0 13 0

' Father Morris is one of the few living writers who have succeeded in greatly modifying certain views of English history, which had long been accepted as the only tenable ones. . . To have wrung an admission of this kind from a reluctant public, never too much inclined to surrender its traditional assumptions, is an achievement not to be underrated in importance."—*Rev. Dr. Augustus Jessopp, in the Academy.*

MORRIS, REV. W. B. (of the Oratory.)

The Life of St. Patrick, Apostle of Ireland. Fourth
edition. Crown 8vo, cloth 0 5 0

"Promises to become the standard biography of Ireland's Apostle. For clear statement of facts, and calm judicious discussion of controverted points, it surpasses any work we know of in the literature of the subject."—*American Catholic Quarterly.*

Ireland and St. Patrick. A study of the Saint's
character and of the results of his apostolate.
Second edition. Crown 8vo, cloth. . . . 0 5 0

"We read with pleasure this volume of essays, which, though the Saint's name is taken by no means in vain, really contains a sort of discussion of current events and current English views of Irish character."—*Saturday Review.*

NEWMAN, CARDINAL.

Church of the Fathers 0 4 0
Prices of other works by Cardinal Newman on
application.

PAGANI, VERY REV. JOHN BAPTIST,

The Science of the Saints in Practice. By John Baptist Pagani, Second General of the Institute of Charity. Complete in three volumes. Vol. 1, January to April (out of print). Vol. 2, May to August. Vol. 3, September to December . each 0 5 0

"'The Science of the Saints' is a practical treatise on the principal Christian virtues, abundantly illustrated with interesting examples from Holy Scripture as well as from the Lives of the Saints. Written chiefly for devout souls, such as are trying to live an interior and supernatural life by following in the footsteps of our Lord and His saints, this work is eminently adapted for the use of ecclesiastics and of religious communities."—*Irish Ecclesiastical Record.*

PAYNE, JOHN ORLEBAR, (M.A.)

Records of the English Catholics of 1715. Demy 8vo.
Half-bound, gilt top 0 15 0

"A book of the kind Mr. Payne has given us would have astonished Bishop Milner or Dr. Lingard. They would have treasured it, for both of them knew the value of minute fragments of historical information. The Editor has derived nearly the whole of the information which he has given, from unprinted sources, and we must congratulate him on having found a few incidents here and there which may bring the old times back before us in a most touching manner."—*Tablet.*

PAYNE, JOHN ORLEBAR, (M.A.)

English Catholic Non-Jurors of 1715. Being a Summary of the Register of their Estates, with Genealogical and other Notes, and an Appendix of Unpublished Documents in the Public Record Office. In one volume. Demy 8vo . . £1 1 0

"Most carefully and creditably brought out ... From first to last, full of social interest and biographical details, for which we may search in vain elsewhere."—*Antiquarian Magazine.*

Old English Catholic Missions. Demy 8vo, half-bound. 0 7 6

"A book to hunt about in for curious odds and ends."—*Saturday Review.*

"These registers tell us in their too brief records, teeming with interest for all their scantiness, many a tale of patient heroism."—*Tablet.*

St. Paul's Cathedral in the time of Edward VI. Being a detailed Account of its Treasures from a Document in the Public Record Office. Tastefully printed on imitation handmade paper, and bound in cloth 0 2 6

PERRY, REV. JOHN,

Practical Sermons for all the Sundays of the year. First and Second Series. Sixth Edition. In two volumes. Cloth 0 7 0

POPE, REV. T. A. (of the Oratory.)

Life of Philip Neri. Translated from the Italian of Cardinal Capecelatro. Second and revised edition. 2 vols, cloth 0 12 6

"Altogether this is a most fascinating work, full of spiritual lore and historic erudition, and with all the intense interest of a remarkable biography. Take it up where you will, it is hard to lay it down. We think it one of the most completely satisfactory lives of a Saint that has been written in modern times."—*Tablet.*

POUVILLON, E.

Bernadette of Lourdes. Translated from the French. By Henry O'Shea. Blue buckram, gilt, . . 0 2 6

"A very charming little miracle-play. It is in the form of prose-narrative, interspersed with dialogue and lyrical snatches; simple, devout, and strewn with tender fancy."—*Weekly Register.*

"A creditable version of a clever and original work."—*Birmingham Daily Gazette.*

QUARTERLY SERIES. Edited by the Rev. John Gerard, S.J. 91 volumes published to date.

Selection.

The Life and Letters of St. Francis Xavier. By the Rev. H. J. Coleridge, S.J. 2 vols. . . . 0 10 6

The History of the Sacred Passion. By Father Luis de la Palma, of the Society of Jesus. Translated from the Spanish. 0 5 0

The Life of Dona Louisa de Carvajal. By Lady Georgiana Fullerton. Small edition . . . 0 3 6

The Life and Letters of St. Teresa. 3 vols. By Rev. H. J. Coleridge, S.J. . . . . . each 0 7 6

The Life of Mary Ward. By Mary Catherine Elizabeth Chalmers, of the Institute of the Blessed Virgin. Edited by the Rev. H. J. Coleridge, S.J. 2 vols. 0 15 0

The Return of the King. Discourses on the Latter Days. By the Rev. H. J. Coleridge, S.J. . . 0 7 6

QUARTERLY SERIES—(*selection*) *continued.*
Pious Affections towards God and the Saints. Meditations for every Day in the Year, and for the Principal Festivals. From the Latin of the Ven. Nicolas Lancicius, S.J. £0 7 6
The Life and Teaching of Jesus Christ in Meditations for Every Day in the Year. By Fr. Nicolas Avancino, S.J. Two vols. 0 10 6
The Baptism of the King: Considerations on the Sacred Passion. By the Rev. H. J. Coleridge, S.J. . . 0 7 6
The Mother of the King. Mary during the Life of Our Lord. 0 7 6
The Hours of the Passion. Taken from the *Life of Christ* by Ludolph the Saxon 0 7 6
The Mother of the Church. Mary during the first Apostolic Age 0 6 0
The Life of St. Bridget of Sweden. By the late F. J. M. A. Partridge 0 6 0
The Teachings and Counsels of St. Francis Xavier. From his Letters 0 5 0
The Life of St. Alonso Rodriguez. By Francis Goldie, of the Society of Jesus . . . 0 7 6
Letters of St. Augustine. Selected and arranged by Mary H. Allies 0 6 6
A Martyr from the Quarter-Deck—Alexis Clerc, S.J. By Lady Herbert 0 5 0
Acts of the English Martyrs, hitherto unpublished. By the Rev. John H. Pollen, S.J. . . . 0 7 6
Life of St. Francis di Geronimo, S.J. By A. M. Clarke. 0 7 6
Aquinas Ethicus; or the Moral Teaching of St. Thomas By the Rev. Joseph Rickaby, S.J. 2 vols. . 0 12 0
The Spirit of St. Ignatius. From the French of the Rev. Fr. Xavier de Franciosi, S.J. . . . 0 6 0
Jesus, the All-Beautiful. A devotional Treatise on the character and actions of Our Lord. Edited by Rev. J. G. MacLeod, S.J. 0 6 6
The Manna of the Soul. By Fr. Paul Segneri. New edition. In two volumes. 0 12 0
Saturday dedicated to Mary. From the Italian of Fr. Cabrini, S.J. 0 6 0
Life of Father Augustus Law, S.J. By Ellis Schreiber. 0 6 0
Life of Ven. Joseph Benedict Cottolengo. From the Italian of Don. P. Gastaldi. 0 4 6
Story of St. Stanislaus Kostka. Edited by Rev. F. Goldie, S.J. 3rd Edition. 0 4 6
Two Ancient Treatises on Purgatory. A Remembrance for the Living to Pray for the Dead, by Father James Mumford, S.J.; and Purgatory Surveyed, by Father Richard Thimelby, S.J. With an Introduction by Rev. J. Morris, S.J. . . 0 5 0
The Lights in Prayer of the Venerable Fathers Louis de la Puente and Claude de la Colombière, and the Rev. Father Paul Segneri. Edited by the Rev. J. Morris, S.J. 0 5 0
Life of St. Francis Borgia. By A. M. Clarke. . 0 6 6

QUARTERLY SERIES—(selection) continued.

	£	s	d
Life of Blessed Antony Baldinucci. By Rev. F. Goldie, S.J.	0	6	0
Distinguished Irishmen of the Sixteenth Century. By Rev. E. Hogan, S. J.	0	6	0
Journals kept during Times of Retreat. By the late Fr. John Morris, S.J. Edited by Rev. J. Pollen, S.J.	0	6	0

VOLUMES ON THE LIFE OF OUR LORD.

The Holy Infancy.

The Preparation of the Incarnation	0	7	6
The Nine Months. The Life of our Lord in the Womb.	0	7	6
The Thirty Years. Our Lord's Infancy and Early Life.	0	7	6

The Public Life of Our Lord.

The Ministry of St. John Baptist	0	6	6
The Preaching of the Beatitudes	0	6	6
The Sermon on the Mount. Continued. 2 Parts, each	0	6	6
The Training of the Apostles. Parts I., II., III., IV. each	0	6	6
The Preaching of the Cross. Part I.	0	6	6
The Preaching of the Cross. Parts II., III. each	0	6	0
Passiontide. Parts I. II. and III., each	0	6	6
Chapters on the Parables of Our Lord	0	7	6

Introductory Volumes.

The Life of our Life. Harmony of the Life of Our Lord, with Introductory Chapters and Indices. Second edition. Two vols.	0	15	0
The Passage of our Lord to the Father. Conclusion of The Life of our Life.	0	7	6
The Works and Words of our Saviour, gathered from the Four Gospels	0	7	6
The Story of the Gospels. Harmonised for Meditation	0	7	6

ROSE, STEWART.

St. Ignatius Loyola and The Early Jesuits, with more than 100 Illustrations by H. W. and H. C. Brewer and L. Wain. The whole produced under the immediate superintendence of the Rev. W. H. Eyre, S.J. Super Royal 8vo. Handsomely bound in cloth, extra gilt. . . . . . net. 0 15 0

"This magnificent volume is one of which Catholics have justly reason to be proud. Its historical as well as its literary value is very great, and the illustrations from the pencils of Mr. Louis Wain and Messrs. H. W. and H. C. Brewer are models of what the illustrations of such a book should be. We hope that this book will be found in every Catholic drawing-room, as a proof that 'we Catholics' are in no way behind those around us in the beauty of the illustrated books that issue from our hands, or in the interest which is added to the subject by a skilful pen and finished style."—*Month.*

RYDER, REV. H. I. D. (of the Oratory.)

Catholic Controversy: A Reply to Dr. Littledale's "Plain Reasons." Seventh edition . . . 0 2 6

"Father Ryder of the Birmingham Oratory, has now furnished in a small volume a masterly reply to this assailant from without. The lighter charms of a brilliant and graceful style are added to the solid merits of this handbook of contemporary controversy."—*Iris Monthly.*

SCHOUPPE, REV. F. X. (S.J.)
  Purgatory. Illustrated by the lives and legends of
    the Saints. Cloth £0 6 0
  " We feel absolutely confident that Father Schouppe's work will
  soon become one of our most popular works on Purgatory, and that
  we shall ere long have to notice its second edition."—*Tablet.*

STANTON, REV. R. (of the Oratory.)
  A Menology of England and Wales ; or, Brief Memorials of the British and English Saints, arranged according to the Calendar. Together with the Martyrs of the 16th and 17th centuries. Compiled by order of the Cardinal Archbishop and the Bishops of the Province of Westminster. With Supplement, containing Notes and other additions, together with enlarged Appendices, and a new Index. Demy 8vo, cloth . 0 16 0
  The Supplement, separately 0 2 0

SWEENEY, RT. REV. ABBOT, (O.S.B.)
  Sermons for all Sundays and Festivals of the Year. Fourth Edition. Crown 8vo, handsomely bound in half leather 0 10 6

THOMPSON, EDWARD HEALY, (M.A.)
  The Life of Jean-Jacques Olier, Founder of the Seminary of St. Sulpice. New and Enlarged Edition. Post 8vo, cloth, pp. xxxvi. 628 . . . . 0 15 0
  " It provides us with just what we most need, a model to look up to and imitate ; one whose circumstances and surroundings were sufficiently like our own to admit of an easy and direct application to our own personal duties and daily occupations."—*Dublin Review.*
  The Life and Glories of St. Joseph, Husband of Mary, Foster-Father of Jesus, and Patron of the Universal Church. Grounded on the Dissertations of Canon Antonio Vitalis, Father José Moreno, and other writers. Second Edition. Crown 8vo, cloth 0 6 0
  Letters and Writings of Marie Lataste, with Critical and Expository Notes. By two Fathers of the Society of Jesus. Translated from the French. 3 vols, ... each 0 5 0

ULLATHORNE ARCHBISHOP.
  Autobiography of, (*see* Drane, A. T.) . . . 0 7 6
  Letters of, do. ,, . . . 0 9 0
  Endowments of Man, &c. Popular edition. . . 0 7 0
  Groundwork of the Christian Virtues : do. . . 0 7 0
  Christian Patience, . . do. do. . . 0 7 0
  Memoir of Bishop Willson 0 2 6

WATERWORTH, REV. J.
  The Canons and Decrees of the Sacred and Œcumenical Council of Trent, celebrated under the Sovereign Pontiffs, Paul III., Julius III., and Pius IV., translated by the Rev. J. WATERWORTH. To which are prefixed Essays on the External and Internal History of the Council. A new edition. Demy 8vo, cloth. 0 10 6

WISEMAN, CARDINAL.
  Fabiola. A Tale of the Catacombs. . . 3s. 6d. and 0 4 0
  Also a new and splendid edition printed on large quarto paper, embellished with thirty-one full-page illustrations, and a coloured portrait of St. Agnes. Handsomely bound 1 1 0

www.ingramcontent.com/pod-product-compliance
Lightning Source LLC
Chambersburg PA
CBHW031402160426
43196CB00007B/863